DETROIT PUBLIC LIBRARY

3 5674 00758101 1

W9-CJF-661

DETROIT PUBLIC LIBRARY

BL

DATE DUE

My Father's House

Also by Meyer Levin

MY FATHER'S HOUSE

BY MEYER LEVIN

NEW YORK · THE VIKING PRESS · 1947

C 3

COPYRIGHT 1947 BY MEYER LEVIN

FIRST PUBLISHED BY THE VIKING PRESS IN AUGUST 1947

PUBLISHED ON THE SAME DAY IN THE DOMINION OF CANADA
BY THE MACMILLAN COMPANY OF CANADA LIMITED

SET IN GRANJON AND GARAMOND TYPES
AND PRINTED IN U.S.A. BY VAIL-BALLOU PRESS
APR 1 7 '63

BL

For

Eli Jonathan Levin

my son

Chapter One

In the hold of the *Hannah Szenesch* few slept. The landing must surely be made this night. They had already lain in the hold twelve days and nights. The darkness was the same, seeming to extend backward into their lives, forming all the days and nights into a single area of time that would now be past.

It would be well if the body would sleep through the remaining interval, until the moment came for being alive. But the body would not sleep.

"We are near. Akiba knows it."

"How does he know it? There is nothing outside but blackness all around."

"He can feel the shore. He is from here."

It didn't matter who spoke. The same words came from all corners. They had been said over and over for many hours. What was said was like the rolling of the ship.

To lie still, as if in sleep, was best, for in the space they had allotted themselves, one lying alongside the other, there was no room for movement. And with less movement, less food and water were required. This was a way of endurance they knew well: it was the ancient torpor of Belsen and Buchenwald which they had assumed again.

They felt no movement of time. They could go on eternally, floating through darkness in the dim womb of the ship. But there was a measure. Each day the water ration grew shorter. It had now come to an end. Thus it was certain that time passed, and now the time was come.

"Try to sleep, David," Marta said as the boy stirred against her and unhuddled his legs.

David had thought that Marta was asleep, she sat so still. Sometimes it took an instant to know the difference; even by her eyes

7

one could not tell for certain. Many times he himself was awake, while his eyes were closed. "I can't sleep any more," he said.

Perhaps he had indeed been asleep and dreaming. He had believed they were aloft, on deck. Two or three times tonight, because he could not sleep, he had gone up on deck, and seen no land, and come down again. Or had he done this in his dreams? No one ever stopped him from going up there, for he was the boy of the ship.

"David, go up and see." It was Blaustein, who always spoke in a hard whisper, as though he were still in the camp, before liberation.

"We are near. I feel it. I am going up myself. I can't wait any more." This came from Ziona. And all around there was a kind of stirring, as though many would go with her.

Swobodniak said, "Even if the English spot the ship, they couldn't see us on the deck in the night." And to convince himself he repeated, "They'll believe it's a fishing ship."

But Lazar, on guard at the bottom of the ladder, said, "They have big searchlights. Do you want us to get caught at the last moment!"

"David, go up and see!"

David made his way along the narrow aisle toward the ladder, feeling carefully with his toes so as not to walk on those who lay on the ship's bottom. With each roll of the ship his body brushed on one side or the other against the tiers of heads and feet, five layers of body over body on each side of him. Sometimes on this voyage when he was in the feeling of half-sleep, it was like being again in the bunkers in the barracks in Buchenwald, when, if you had to go out at night, you had to pass between the tiers of bodies and faces lying on the shelves, one on top of the other.

In the daytime, since he was one who could go up on the outside of the ship as much as he wanted, it was easier for him to remember the open places, the times on the roads just after the Americans came, the times of being able to go anywhere at all.

Near the ladder hung the small lantern, and David could see Lazar's face, with the beard he was growing in order to make himself look like a man. In the tight space around the ladder several people sat, breathing the air. The small hatch was half open, and David could see night clouds and a few stars through the slit. He

8

shouldered it further open and climbed out on the deck. It was cool. There was a touch of wind.

He took a new breath, and had to wait a moment until his body was used to the air, as always when coming out of the bottom, for down there it was not like air, but like a dough that was one mass with the people, all having one smell. Whenever he came out, the real air always made him a little dizzy. Breathing was like learning to breathe, and the air came into places in the body where the other air was too thick to reach.

Giant Stepan was lucky, as always; he was on guard tonight.

"Have you seen it yet?" David asked.

"If I see it, I'll swim," Stepan promised.

David considered whether he should swim alongside of the Giant. He was not sure he could swim well enough; but all the way from Buchenwald Stepan had never left him behind.

Now David moved forward, knowing the ship, until he came to the passage around the wheelhouse. The sick one, Weisbrod, wrapped in an extra coat, lay against the wall of the little cabin, beside the girls who were going to have babies, babies who would be born in Palestine. In the wheelhouse, David saw Akiba was steering, while still wearing the radio earphones. The Italian captain dozed in the canvas chair.

"Aha! He is here!" Akiba said in his usual growl. "No, you can't tell them anything yet, down there."

"They said you know we are near because you can feel the bottom of the sea."

"Yes, I am made of radar," Akiba said.

"Will we land tonight?"

"Soon, *chabibi*," Akiba said gravely. "Soon the *Hannah Szenesch* will be home." And though he always spoke seriously even when he was joking, David believed he saw a difference in Akiba's face.

"Can you tell where we are?" David asked, excited.

"I can smell it. I smell the orange groves."

David tried to smell, but it seemed the same. Akiba was joking. Then maybe he was joking about everything, the landing, too. In the bottom of the ship Swobodniak had said there were vessels that never came to Palestine, but ended in Syria and in Greece, or amid unknown islands.

"Did you get a signal?" David asked.

Akiba nodded.

"Can you tell exactly where we are?"

Akiba shrugged. Then he patted the wheel. "But *Hannah* knows. She's going right home."

David was not entirely sure he could trust this idea. If the ship had really been built in Akiba's own colony, she might know her way home; but even though she was a small ship, Akiba had told him, she was larger than what they could so far build. So she was not truly from home, she had never been here before, she was only the Italian's fishing ship, the *Guiseppa*. And though they secretly knew her name had been changed, and that her true name was now the name of a heroine, Hannah Szenesch, the old name was still painted on her bow. David could read the letters himself, when he hung over the side in the daytime, for Stepan and the others had taught him to read a little from the letters that were on the American tins of food.

But sometimes he wondered if the ship could really have been changed from the *Guiseppa* to the *Hannah Szenesch*. For it was like people who carried false cards with false names. Marta said they remained the same.

Akiba had a joke about the ship's name. "As long as she smelled of fish," he said, "she was the *Guiseppa*. But now our own smell is stronger, so she is ours."

David asked about the heroine, Hannah Szenesch, although he knew the story well. "Was she a girl from here?"

"From here. From my own colony. I knew her." And Akiba repeated the tale of the girl parachutist who had dropped into Hungary to fight alongside the Jews of the underground, with the mission of bringing them home to Palestine. He told again how she had been captured and shot. Nevertheless, Akiba said, Hannah's mission would now be fulfilled. That was why the ship carried her name.

"If the English catch us now," David repeated to Akiba, "we will fight them." And then he asked, "If they capture us, will they shoot us?"

"Only one or two, by accident," Akiba said.

"Are they looking for us? With radar?"

"With radar, *chabibaleh*," Akiba said.

"And they also have patrol boats, which go very fast."

"It's a good night for landing," Akiba said. "So far we are lucky."

Marta had come up after David. She was standing against the wall of the cabin.

David felt impelled to repeat the story of the heroine. Sometimes he felt as though this boat were her body, carrying them all to her shore. "Hannah was killed. They shot her," he said.

"Yes," Marta said, "I know."

Stepan wanted to be the first to see the land, to see it even before Akiba, who knew it so well. His huge cropped head, his big-boned form, projected over the rail. The ship was rolling heavily. It was difficult to tell whether there was any forward movement, because there was no mark to check against. The ship rolled like a cradle under an agitated hand.

Then Stepan saw, or felt, the land. It was like standing on guard in a forest somewhere and realizing that someone has been standing near you for some time. At first you shudder, and then, recognizing that it is one of your own people, a friend, you take ease from the presence.

The land was like a low, concentrated part of the general darkness. Stepan lurched to the cabin, crying, "It's there!" Akiba merely nodded, he had already seen it, and in the nod there was also an admonition against loud excitability. Still, Stepan would not let himself believe Akiba had actually seen it first. Perhaps at the same moment.

David stayed close to big Stepan. The sick ones began to raise their heads and turn in their positions. The French girl, Tessa, who was watching them, tried to describe the sight to those who could not move.

"What does it look like, our land?"

"Like it is waiting for us in the dark."

How they knew, below, was how all things become known. First Lazar himself, noticing the stir above, left his post and climbed up the ladder. And now the people began to bubble upward, and neither Lazar nor Stepan halted them. Ziona, and young Dvora, and Blaustein crawled out on the deck, then others, and more. They moved to the rail. They whispered, and wanted to sing, and were hushed. The ship seemed to be moving only sidewise, rocking closer to the land.

"They have signaled to Akiba on the radio."

"How do we know where they are?"

"They may be a hundred miles away."

"Akiba knows the shore. He knows where they are."

"It was in the plan. A point near Caesarea."

"If we don't find them, we'll land by ourselves."

They waited. This was the hardest time of all.

Stepan went again to Akiba. "Let me swim," Stepan insisted. "I'm a good swimmer. I can find them. I'll find them and tell them we are here."

"Wait," Akiba said. He would try to go in close enough so that those on shore might see the ship. He could not send them a message. His radio was no longer sending.

On the shore the forward men of the party were posted, covering the landing area. They were from four different settlements. The radioman, Zev Feldheim, was back in the orange grove, near the truck. He had walked with such a radio all the way to El Alamein. In those years it had grown like a hump to his back. He had not thought he would ever walk upright again. But every experience in life could be useful, Zev believed. He had taken this radio apart and rebuilt it himself. He knew it was all right.

"I can't receive anything," he said. "I don't believe they are sending."

Amos was his runner. It was the boy's first time on a landing, and he was excited. Maybe they were not sending for fear of interception, he suggested.

"Akiba is from here," Zev repeated, for himself as well as for Amos. "He'll find us."

Amos hurried back to the beach to report to Avram.

Avram was sitting against a rock, his jacket loose over his shoulders. One more hour, he thought, and they would have to give up and hide the landing boats. There would not be time enough to complete the landing before the predawn light. Though an army patrol need not be expected so early, who could tell when some

Arab would come wandering down, for no reason—and it might be an Arab who would say nothing, and it might be an Arab who would run to the English for a reward, for baksheesh.

Then all at once there was the shape of a ship. Moshe tapped him and pointed. It was detaching itself from the farther dark, coming a little closer. Avram waited until he could be sure of the two little masts. Nothing could be taken for granted in these times; they might even try a decoy to catch the landing party. But the masts were as described.

He took his flashlight from his pocket; it was a good American army torch. Then he flashed two dots for the signal, the letter B, standing for the dark immigration that was called Immigration B, *Aliyah Beth*. And through his mind there crossed the idea that it also stood for the word *bayit*—house, home.

Moshe was already pushing his boat out from behind the rocks. The younger boys, working like veterans, moved out the next two boats. Avram sent word to the guards at the edges of the landing area. The operation was beginning. There was no going away now. Yehudith came closer to the water's edge, with her first-aid kit. Avram waded out and climbed into the first boat.

They flowed up on deck now, thrusting up their rucksacks and bundles. "Silently, silently, discipline!" the section leaders whispered to their units, trying to form them into boatloads. But a delirium was upon the ship. In the dark, in the tiny deckspace, it was impossible to keep to plan.

Now they heard oars dipping in the water, like footsteps coming toward them. "I can't wait!" Stepan whispered, and then, in the Hebrew they had begun to learn, he added, *"L'hitra-oth-ba-Aretz*—I'll see you in Eretz Yisroel!" And he slid over the rail and into the water.

David would have climbed after big Stepan, but he felt a hand touching him. It was Marta. She was always near enough to touch him.

"Look, a man is bringing the boat for us," she said.

Then he could even see the boat, and a man standing upright at the prow. David shivered. It was as if he had known he would see it exactly in this way. And Marta had known what was in his thoughts. As the boat came, crossing the waves, it rose and de-

scended, and the man with it, each time as though going into the
sea and rising from the sea.

"It's just as I told you!" David whispered to Marta. "I think it
must be my father. He is coming to meet me, just as I told you!"
Now he could see the man more clearly. There was a coil of rope
around his shoulder, and he was holding the end in his hand.

Even before the boat arrived David knew how it would touch
the side of their vessel, and then the man would call up to them,
"Is David Halevi among you?" And then, David knew, he would
answer, and he would jump over the rail, to the man in the boat
below.

But Marta was looking into his face, in the way she had, without saying anything. Perhaps it was not his father who had flashed
the signal with the light. Perhaps it was not his father standing in
the first boat. But surely his father was waiting there, on the shore,
in the dark. This Marta would see.

Up to the last moment there were those who were not sure.

"It could still be a trick of the police to catch us," Swobodniak
said. He held an iron bar in his hand, in readiness.

Akiba left the wheelhouse and came up behind them, to the
rail. Akiba's face was new—he was smiling altogether. "Their
police don't need such tricks," he said. "They just send a few de-
stroyers and ram you."

Now the man in the prow of the small boat flung his rope, and
a hundred hands caught at it, but David was sure it came directly
to him, and he was the first to seize hold of it. He pulled, and they
all pulled, and the small boat rubbed alongside of the *Hannah
Szenesch*. They saw other boats coming directly behind it. A voice
whispered up to them, *"Shalom, Yehudim!* Peace, Jews!"

"Avram!" Akiba knew him.

David saw that the man on the boat, Avram, was wearing a
soldier's jacket. He was a Palestinian, like Akiba, only he was
more cheerful.

"Are you all right?" Avram asked Akiba. "We've watched
three nights for you. Why didn't you talk to us?"

"We're all right. My sender went out."

"Akiba, you'll have to get them off quickly. We're taking some
of them all the way to Makor Gallil." Avram's whisper became
louder now, to include all of them. "Comrades, absolute quiet.

14

Move quickly. We've only a few boats. Those who can, get into the water and hold on."

Even while he spoke the group leaders were letting down ropes and putting ladders over the side. David was among the first to plunge down to the waiting boat. It rocked away from the ship, and he swung himself out on the rope, so as not to fall in the water. Strong hands caught him.

Then he stood beside the one called Avram and reached up to help others get into the boat. He took Marta's blanket, and caught Dvora's pack, and people poured into the boat, while others let themselves into the water and clung to the sides. All around there were the small sounds of people dropping into the water like stones.

As the boat pushed away from the ship, David saw many swimming alongside, and others trailing on Avram's rope; among them he saw Lazar, his young beard all wet against his face. David seized hold of the long fisherman's oar and pulled, together with Avram and many other hands.

Stepan had kicked off all of his clothes; he was naked in the water. He felt stronger than ever in his life; with each stroke he felt as though he were seizing the land and pulling it toward him. It was not so far; he would be the first. He would touch it alone, by himself, first.

Now he could feel the bottom. It was covered with small sharp stones; that was fitting, he wanted it so, instead of a smooth beach. He stumbled and pressed through the water, letting the stones cut his feet. With his arms and legs and his whole body he flung himself to the land.

The water flowed away from him, leaving him clear on the beach of stones. But under the stones there was earth. His huge tough hands swept away the stones, seized the damp soil. He held the soil in his fist and felt like laughing. He was here! He was here!

Two young people came running toward him—one was a girl, with a white armband; there was no cross on it, but a star. Stepan stood up, grinning, still holding his handful of earth.

"*Shalom, shalom!*" they cried, and seeing he needed no help, they ran on, knee-deep into the water, to pull in the boats. Stepan turned and waded out with them to the boats, like a Palestinian, helping the new ones to land.

As the prow scraped bottom Avram leaped over the side to pull in the boat. David jumped after him. But he had not thought that the Palestinian was so tall; a wave rolled in upon them, and David was in the water to his neck, though it reached only to Avram's waist. The boy stumbled on the sharp stones, and water came over his head, and the waves were pulling his feet from under him, pulling him back away from the land.

Then someone lifted him out of the sea. It was the Palestinian, Avram, raising him up on his shoulders and pushing through the sea. David saw Marta and the others just behind them, wet and stumbling on the sharp stones. Then Avram set him down on the land.

David looked quickly about, but he saw only the faces of the people from the boat as they came crowding ashore, hurrying to reunite with each other, and some of them hurrying back to help their friends who were still in the water.

David turned to the Palestinian. Avram was very tall, and more like a soldier than a father. He wore no hat. Even in the darkness David could tell that his face was different from those of the Europeans, just as in Europe the faces of Americans had been different. And yet in that first moment of seeing Avram on the prow of the boat, David had felt that this man had to be his father whom he had come to find. But Avram had not called out to him. It could not be Avram.

The place was stony, and there were large rocks close to the water. Against one rock David saw a guard with a tommy gun. He was a heavier man; he was not in uniform but wore an old coat and a cloth hat. He looked older, more like a father of children. But he was not looking for anyone; he was only on guard.

David turned to Avram. "Isn't my father here?" he asked.

"Who?"

"My father told me he would meet me in Palestine," David explained.

Marta was standing with them now, and David saw Avram look to her as though she could explain things better. Avram must surely think he belonged to Marta. David wanted to tell Avram that she was not of his family, that she was only a friend from the boat.

But Avram was replying to him, "You know, this meeting place is secret. We had to ask all the families to wait until we had you safely landed. Even your father."

"Then you know my father?" David said eagerly. "I'm David, David Halevi." But he saw that the man did not know how to answer him, and then David felt that something was wrong, for surely his father would not be kept out of a secret. Perhaps even this Palestinian was not to be trusted.

"David, you're soaked!" Marta cried. "Here, take off your jacket."

It was his combat jacket that a soldier named Benny had given him right after Buchenwald. The winning soldiers were good, they always had too much food. They had given him their stripes and emblems for the jacket, and said they wanted to take him to America. Even when people seemed good, you could not let them do what they wanted with you; they never could understand that his family was in Palestine. Now, as Avram reached to take off the dripping coat, David pulled away from him. "An American soldier gave it to me," he said.

Avram took off his own battle jacket; it had a blue star on the sleeve, and sergeant's stripes. "Here, keep dry, *chabibi,*" he said.

The three boats were already unloaded; Avram saw the last sick ones being carried ashore. That would complete his section. Avram signaled to Amos to clear this part of the beach and get the people to the trucks. They would be the first out if the sick didn't hold them up. He checked with the first-aid girl, Yehudith. She was leaning over a skeleton with stretched gray skin; the man kept putting a rag to his mouth, wiping away blood.

"I shouldn't have come, I'll only be a burden," he kept muttering.

It was an exhaustion case; probably scurvy. Yehudith was giving him tablets that would stop the bleeding.

Avram motioned to Moshe to help Yehudith get the sick one to the truck. Then he hurried along with the first of them, up the steep embankment, quickly herding their dark shapes across the half mile of wasteland to the grove.

The boy kept right along with him. Avram glanced to his rear. The young naked giant had found a pair of shorts and was helping carry the sick one. Amos came along on the run, reporting that all was clear. Avram sent the youth on ahead to alert Zev and the truck driver Chayim.

Thus far, luck was good.

Zev was waiting at the edge of the grove.

Young Amos reported breathlessly, "They're all off the ship! We made it!"

Zev smiled his dim, slightly sour smile at the excited youth. There was still the long ride home, and though there was no curfew on the road just now, one might always run into a roving scout car, curious about the covered load in the truck. The sentence for aiding illegals could run up to eight years, provided there was no fight, no shooting. Or if they even found a gun, that could mean a life in prison—or execution. And in the same instant Zev saw his children grown, without him, little Shulamith a long-legged beauty walking toward the dining-hall in the settlement. But, oddly enough, he couldn't think of the baby as anything but a baby. He caught himself, amused at his habitual pessimistic projections.

Zev and Amos walked to the truck to stow away the radio. Amos was continuing enthusiastically, and almost with the tone of a veteran and expert of such landings. "They look like a good bunch, mostly young, lots of partisans among them, good material!"

Zev sensed what the boy was thinking. Amos belonged to a youth group that was in training at the settlement, waiting to go onto their own land. Surely Amos was already dreaming about incorporating some of the newcomers into his group, to fill it out, and surely the boy was already envisioning how they, the Palestinians, would melt in their energy with the refugees' and carry the refugees into a new life.

The first of the arrivals broke through the screen of tall young cypress that served as fence and windbreak for the grove. They came in a bunch, their soaked, broken shoes gathering mud in the light soil. Zev noticed that they were mostly short, stunted, the survivors, but no longer starved looking; many had become sturdy. And among the young women he noticed a few who were pregnant. Yes, this was a good group, the comrades had not forgotten even this stratagem for bringing more souls into Israel.

Amos and Zev extended their arms to lift the young women onto the truck.

Avram left the column of refugees and hurried to the front end of the vehicle. Chayim was ready at the wheel, and he had the motor turning. Avram ducked partway into the cab of the truck and illuminated his watch for a second; it would be better, for things like this, to get himself one with a luminous dial. It was half-past one.

"How was the fishing?" Chayim asked.

"Good, good," Avram said. "More than we can carry."

"It's nearly two." Chayim emphasized the lateness, looking apprehensively at Avram. The whole calculation was behind his glance, beginning with tours they had made in the desert together, from the first time they had navigated the trackless sand toward Tobruk, and the time with the load of landmines that were to be placed in Rommel's path, knowing the strafing that would come if you were still a moving object on the road, after dawn.

Now there was the same calculation, to reach the objective before dawn, and part of the way with blackout driving.

"We'll lose half an hour taking the back road," Avram said. But still they could not chance going through Haifa. Unless boldly, with the lights on.

"How fast can you get them loaded?" Chayim asked.

"Two minutes." It would be the last part of the trip that would be difficult. They could avoid the Beisan road and the police inspection at Gesher only by taking the way through the hills, through Yavneel. But to make the hills, with the old truck and the heavy load— Avram glanced at Chayim. They were thinking of the same problem.

"Even if the British got wind of the landing, they would be unlikely to check the hills around Yavneel," Chayim said.

That was true; the British would not search so far inland from the sea. They would most likely search the usual colonies, Sdot Yam and Yagur.

"Was it Akiba?" Chayim asked.

"Akiba himself. I didn't have a chance to talk to him. He's going right back."

Chayim raced his motor, just enough for a hint. Avram hurried to the back of the truck.

Zev and Amos were loading the refugees as fast as possible, and the refugees were scarcely lingering. They pressed around the back of the truck, waiting their turn to climb aboard. Their discipline was good; Avram had already seen this on the beach.

The big lad who had been in such a hurry to swim ashore had discovered the last oranges of the season, still on the trees. With one hand he stuffed an orange to his mouth, biting into the skin, while with his other hand he pulled down more fruit, for his comrades.

The child David took the round yellow fruit questioningly. "What is it, Stepan?" he asked.

"An orange! An orange of Judea." The big one, Stepan, spat out a section of the skin and bit enthusiastically into the fruit.

Again Avram caught the eyes of the dark young woman who was watching the boy. One could not enter her eyes, they were opaque; her eyes did not share anything with him, but they linked him to her preoccupation with the boy. Avram let himself take an instant's satisfaction at the sight of the child, now engulfed in his own brigade coat.

"Up, children!" he hurried them. "You'll have all your lives to pick oranges!"

David turned the fruit in his palms. Now that he heard the name, an orange, he recognized the fruit, and by the feel of it, he thought he remembered long ago having known such a fruit. Long ago, from the hands of his mother. He could not remember the taste of it.

Everyone was mounting the truck. Even Lazar, still shaking himself like a wet dog, swung aloft.

"Up, up!" the Palestinian kept saying.

David knew it was different here: there were no guns pushing you into boxcars, no guns forcing you onto the backs of trucks that were going nobody knew where.

But where were they going? Where were they taking him? And how would anybody know where to find him?

20

"But we're going to our settlement," Avram answered the boy, "to Makor Gallil." The woman stood there passively; surely she could see there was no time for him to explain everything to children.

"Will we stay there long?" the boy asked.

"You'll live there with us," Avram said. "Up, son!" And he took the boy under the elbows, to boost him into the truck.

David would not budge. "I can't go," he said.

There was no time, there was no time for problems. But, as before, the woman's eyes insistently linked him to the child. Patiently Avram asked the boy, "Why can't you go?"

"I have to find my father," David explained. "My father said I would find the whole family here in Palestine."

Then that was why she was standing there, as though to emphasize that even in this urgent moment he had to learn about this boy. The child's face was so serious. Avram spoke to him lightly. "You have to find him now? In the middle of the night?"

And at last the young woman helped. She touched David's shoulder. "We can't keep everybody waiting, David," she said. "We might all get caught. In the morning we can ask about your family."

"*Yallah!* Up, *chabibi!*" Avram gave the child a little boost as he climbed into the truck.

The pill that the first-aid girl had given him tasted slightly astringent. Weisbrod recognized the ingredients. But the mouth-bleeding continued. He could have asked her for a coagulator. She probably had something in her kit. But he did not ask. It was the same with him as it had been on the ship, and before, in the liberated camps. He could have asked for vitamins. There would have been no scurvy, no bleeding now. But he had not asked.

The young giant Stepan carried him as far as the truck, holding him across his arms as one carries a very young child. Stepan set him down gently, and the first-aid girl looked again at his bleeding. Everyone was already on the truck; he was delaying things.

"Never mind, never mind," Weisbrod said. "It isn't worth the trouble." He struggled halfway to his feet, and the boy lifted him into the truck.

21

Amos slapped up the backboard, and Avram helped him pull the tarpaulin over and tie it. They hopped up on the driver's seat, next to Chayim.

"Three in front," Chayim grumbled, to remind them that this was a violation of the traffic law.

Amos laughed adventurously at Chayim's scruple.

"That's just enough for them to stop us," Chayim pointed out. "Then they decide to have a look inside, and *halas!* Finish!"

Avram shrugged. "They'll get us first for driving without lights."

Chayim moved the old vehicle gently, carefully, out of the grove, so as not to injure the trees. Theirs was the first truck to leave. So much the better; they had the farthest to go. He gave her power, feeling the wheels churn through the sand ruts. He leaned forward intently, listening and feeling for other vehicles, just as he had in the desert, before El Alamein, years ago.

The truck rocked like the ship rocking. The immigrants were crowded together. There was not enough room for all of them to sit or lie, and many stood, grasping the structure for support. They rolled and rocked against one another, as they had done on so many trucks, on so many roads, and on the sea. It was strange to think and hard to believe that this was the final part of the voyage, and that this time they were upon their own land. And even now in the last part of their voyage there was frustration, for they could not see their land. Even in the darkness they could not come openly.

Some of them, like Swobodniak, could not yet rule out of their minds the fantasies of disbelief. He whispered his eternal suspicions to Lazar. How could one be sure it was Palestine? How could one even be sure these were Jews? Hadn't there been tales of ships that had landed by error or by treason on Cyprus and in Syria? And could it still not be, even if they had landed in Palestine, that the entire landing party was a hoax, and this truck, all enclosed and sealed, would carry their bodies only to another gate of iron, and they would find themselves within another barbed-wire camp, such as existed in Palestine, too?

Lazar scarcely listened to the endless nightmare. He avoided the narrow, blinking little eyes. He was squeezed against Stepan on the other side, and little Dvora, half asleep, was leaning against Stepan.

They had talked with the envoys in the camps about Palestine, until they had thought they would know it, every inch of it. Especially Stepan; he had learned to discourse about the Emek and the Negev like an expert.

"Can you tell where we are?" Lazar whispered to Stepan. It was as though through the wheels of the truck they might feel the contours of their land as they passed.

The Palestinian named Zev was standing like a center-pole in the middle of the vehicle, holding on to a crossbar of the roof. He was older than the first one, Avram, and also very tall. Zev leaned over to speak to them. He never whispered, unlike the others; there was something in his manner that would not yield as far as whispering. His voice was full but low. "We are on Mount Carmel," Zev informed them.

"Carmel!" Stepan repeated the word to young Dvora, and her head nodded drowsily as though the image had become part of her dream.

The boy David reclined against Marta, his head on her knees. No one had been there on the beach for him, and now he was being carried away. All the time on the ship he had thought that he was being carried to them, but now he felt that he would sometime have to return over every foot of this distance that he was being carried. He could see himself as he would be walking the road with Giant Stepan, just as they had walked the roads in Europe. Stepan would come with him.

David knew he was still in the dark truck, and yet in his dream he was going around a big table. The table was very high, so that he could just manage to see the dishes that were part of the feast. In order to partake of the feast he would have to sit on someone's lap. All around the table big people sat, and he was going around the table, to someone, to sit on someone's knees.

There was a shelf rigged up against the side of the truck, and upon this they had placed Weisbrod. Yehudith squatted near him. She was watching him, and also watching one of the pregnant women, who gasped with every jolt of the truck. In Weisbrod's mind there came a fantasy in which the pregnant girl began to have

23

labor pains. He judged her seven months. Her teeth were decayed. She needed calcium. In his fantasy the truck halted, and she was placed on the grass by the wayside, where she began to give birth. There was a complication. The infant was partly delivered, and half strangled in the cord. He saw what it was and saw what to do. With his hands he could surely deliver it. His hands were dirty. But in the first-aid bag there was surely some alcohol. But his hands would not move. And nothing within him moved to help the mother and child. It was as though he were under a wall of glass, and through this wall he was watching them. He simply lay still, and watched them, and, like all the others he had watched in his years of lying on the boards in the *lagers,* this mother and child also died, while he did not lift his hands.

The first-aid girl peeled an orange that someone had brought into the truck. She offered him half, but he turned his face away, and she gave it all to the pregnant one.

Chayim ground slowly over the back of Mount Carmel and came down to the Emek. On the left there was an encampment of the Arab legion, from Trans-Jordan. But as he had thought, they did not care to keep guards awake to trouble the roads all night long. He passed it and went smoothly through the valley.

It was after four when they came to the crossroads and had to decide, for the last time, between the low road and the hills. The truck was making a whole combination of noises.

"Can she make the hills again?" Avram wondered.

Chayim halted, got out, and poured water from the spare tin into the radiator. Once more they decided for the hills.

They already felt the light of predawn as they went by Tabor. The top of the little mountain was enveloped in clouds, which were like a whirl of rough silvery hair. It would have been something for them to see, those behind, in there.

As they came through the pass toward Yavneel, Arabs were already moving about, with their goats and sheep. Chayim put her into low for the last climb. Avram passed his cigarettes. They felt safer, almost at home now.

In the body of the truck Zev told them the name of the place. He knew it well, for here he had been born, and he knew every foot of the rocky hill upon which his father and the other Lovers of Zion who had come from Berdichev had struggled so stubbornly. The remains of the old colony would be off to the left, on the summit; only a few broken walls of the long-abandoned buildings were to be seen, for the Lovers of Zion had lost too many crops for lack of water.

The truck had only to coast down this winding mountain, and then they would be home.

Suddenly Chayim braked the truck.

The immigrants rolled and tumbled against one another. Yehudith caught Weisbrod just as he was about to fall from his shelf. One of the refugee girls, the rough-haired Ziona, peered through the back window of the cab. She saw two camels rising up in the road before the truck.

"Arabs!" she cried. There was a belligerence, almost a triumph, in her voice that the danger had come so soon.

"We're caught after all," Swobodniak said.

They were all awake on the instant, and Zev could feel the violence that came from them. Enemies were the rule of life, enemies would be met at every instant, at every turn, and they had fought to come this far, and they would fight.

Zev managed to get a glimpse through a corner of the little window, over the driver's shoulder. It was only a neighboring Arab, Jamal, plodding home from a market somewhere with his two camels and his boy and his donkey, and they must have sat down in the road to rest.

Avram had already hopped off the truck to exchange greetings with the Arab.

"It's only Jamal, from our neighboring village," Zev explained to those inside.

But the word Arab had gone through the truck, and they were still uneasy, repeating, "Won't he tell on us?"

Zev laughed to steady them. "First," he said, "Jamal doesn't even know you are here. And second, he is our neighbor. With our neighbors we get along."

"You can't trust an Arab," one of the newcomers said knowingly.

Again Zev laughed his short, melancholy laugh. "That may be true," he said, "but still, you know, they retained some of our

25

prophets in their religion, and they follow the words of Solomon"
—he quoted to them in his deliberate, schoolmasterish voice, " 'De-
vise not trouble against thy neighbor, with whom thou livest in
security.' "

One or two of them looked wisely up at Zev, to show him they
understood that the meaning cut in two directions, and the
bearded young partisan, Lazar, repeated, as though he were already an old settler, "The Arabs know from experience—if they
give us trouble, they will get back more than they give!"

Not all of the immigrants felt reassured. "But isn't there trouble
with them?" Blaustein insisted. "Haven't you had trouble?"

"Yes, we've had our difficulties," Zev said. They would learn
the complications in their time: whom to believe, and whom to
bribe, and whom to fear; they would learn not to think of the
Arab as a wild savage hiding by the roadside with a knife in his
teeth, but as a poor bondsman, working his bit of land, supersti-
tious, full of guile, and yet often of true honor, but easily misled.
"We've had trouble with some of them," Zev repeated. "They
usually come from outside. But Jamal's village is all right."

"We're safe now," Yehudith said. "We're on Jewish land."

David had come fully awake and had placed himself by the
little window to see what was happening. There were camels, as
people had said there would be. In the dim light these animals
looked unbelievable. There was also an Arab in a long gown, with
a kerchief tied around his head; he was pulling the camels, and
an Arab boy was pulling a donkey off the road so that the truck
could pass.

He wondered why they went on the roads at night. "Is it like
in the war?" he asked. "Do people travel at night because of the
fighting?"

"No, *chabibi,*" Zev said, chuckling. "They travel at night only
because the days are so hot, here in the valley, for this is one of the
hottest parts of Palestine. So the Arabs walk at night."

David watched the Arab boy climb upon the donkey.

"They're going away!" Ziona called victoriously.

While the others had crowded to the little window Stepan had
pulled up the tarpaulin at the back of the truck, partly with the

instinct for having a way out in case there was trouble, and partly because he felt the light of predawn and needed to see the land. Stepan put his big cropped head out from under the canvas, and a sound must have escaped him, for in a moment young Dvora's face was beside his, and then the others were around him, Lazar, and David, and Swobodniak.

The truck stood on the bend of a sharply winding road, and below them, milky in the earliest light, was their land and their lake. The land lay open, and the few settlements below were like the beginning of writing in one corner of a sheet of paper, and beyond stretched the gray barren valley.

The sight freed them. Stepan leaped from the truck, and Dvora and David and half a dozen others tumbled after him, while many faces filled the open end of the truck. Even the Palestinians climbed down, and Zev and Yehudith stood with them as they enjoyed their first sight of the land.

"There is our settlement, on the little hill, not far from the lake," Yehudith said. They saw it, far down, as a pattern of small white rectangles for the houses, and a pattern of colors for the fields, reaching to the pale quiet lake, and on the far side of the lake they saw the red wall of the Trans-Jordan cliffs, with the break of light coming from behind them.

Young Dvora remembered pictures of such a sea, and of white-robed figures walking along its shores. "It looks like pictures of the Sea of Galilee, among the Christians," she said.

"We call it Kinneret," Yehudith said.

Zev explained to them, "In Hebrew, *kinor* means a violin."

"Because of its shape," Yehudith added, "or some say because of the sound of the waves."

Avram had come around to the back of the truck. He stood with them for a moment, to let the sight fill their eyes. "Up, up, comrades," he said, laughing.

They kept the tarpaulin open at the rear of the truck, and as they rolled down the steep hill Yehudith began to sing the song of the lake:

"... and perhaps it was not just a dream,
Oh, Kinneret, Kinneret of mine ..."

27

Their faces were all around her. Many of them picked up the tune, humming, and some, who had learned enough Hebrew in the camps where they had waited, picked up the words:

"*Ay, Kinneret, Kinneret sheli . . .*"

Their voices became firmer, stronger. She felt young, and proud of her mission—at last, Yehudith thought, they are free to sing.

Chapter Two

The settlement of Makor Gallil was built on a rise of ground overlooking the Sea of Galilee. Its fields reached back toward the hills and were cut off at the foot of the hills by the River Jordan. The river, winding in a labyrinth, spread shallow at each bend. There were many places where the Arabs of Abiyah, the opposite hill village, tucking up their robes, followed their donkeys across the water; then they would pass through the fields of Makor Gallil on their way to Tiberias.

Before dawn the settlers were awake and at their tasks, working through the cool hours until breakfast. But on such a morning, when the active nucleus of the Hagana was out on a mission, a general tension pervaded the commune. The younger ones would not permit themselves to feel it as anxiety. They grumbled that they too were not on the mission with Avram. But the family heads, as they walked through the dark on the familiar paths to the dining-hall for a pre-breakfast mug of tea and bread, as they fell alongside of comrades whom they recognized by their long-familiar shapes and voices, these older ones repeated the reassuring litany that once a ship got through to the beach, the English so far had never been there, or had had the good sense to look the other way during the landings, and surely this one would come off without trouble too. In any case, they repeated, Avram and Zev knew how to handle themselves.

These "older ones," the heads of families, were not very old. They were mostly like Zev, bordering thirty, on one side or the other, for Makor Gallil was a young commune. They had come as a youth group to this place, and built it in these ten years; their school went thus far only to the third grade. But now, in their turn, they were the "older ones," for they had a youth group training among them.

Setting down their empty tea mugs, the comrades reassured each other that it was a long drive, that under the best circumstances the truck could not be expected to arrive until dawn, that there was no cause for worry, that, indeed, if anything had gone wrong, there would have been a telephone alarm by now.

There were a few truly older ones in the commune, parents of the settlers, such as Zipporah the worrier. She had come to the kitchen an hour earlier than was her turn, to superintend extra breakfast preparations for the newcomers.

And Abba, the father of Avram, had pestered the work committee for watchman's duty this night. Hillel, the secretary, had resisted, concerned about Abba's malaria. To ride about all night, exposed to the mosquitoes from the swamp, was no assignment for the old pioneer. And what use would his vigil be, since the truck was not expected before dawn? Nevertheless, Abba insisted. His old hide was too tough for the little mosquitoes of the present generation, he declared, and somehow he got his way. Wearing the traditional Arab *keffia* of the old-time night watchmen, he was riding about on Gedalia, the settlement's best horse. Abba did not permit himself to go far beyond the fields of Makor Gallil, for after all a night watchman had his duty; he rode only as far as the nest of black Bedouin tents, toward Yavneel, for where there were Bedouin there were thieves. Twice he saw headlights on the road and galloped toward them, though he was not sure Chayim would be using his headlights, even so close to home. They proved to be army trucks.

The third time Abba saw the shape of the old truck for certain; her canvas was billowing like an old woman's skirts. Patting his palm against his open mouth to sound a far-echoing Arab fantasia-cry, Abba galloped toward the truck, and his *keffia* streamed behind him in the wind.

The three who were riding in front laughed as the old man reined up beside them. "So you did it!" he yelled to Avram. "Even without me!"

"Did you think I wouldn't?" Avram called back to him.

Abba was beaming like the morning sun. "You didn't forget to bring a few beautiful girls?" he joked.

"Am I your son or not?" Avram retorted.

The old man pulled off his Arab kerchief, wheeled, and raced across the fields with his happy news. His white hair stood up in a circle.

They watched him fondly. Truly the early settlers rode like Arabs.

On the watchtower Hillel, the secretary, was on duty. He saw Abba's white halo, and the next moment caught sight of the silhouette of the truck along the road by the lakeside. Hillel cupped his hands to his mouth. "They're here, they're here! They made it!" he yelled.

In the yard a comrade, passing the dining-hall, seized the clapper and sounded the gong.

Nahama, the wife of Zev Feldheim, had heard every sound during the night. Twice she had heard the watchman when he had clattered into the yard and dismounted by the kitchen for a mug of hot tea; and all night the jackals had seemed louder than ever. Just before dawn little Shulamith had crept from the children's house, to be with her mother, and then they had gone to get the baby, so that all would be together when Zev came. They were in the infants' house when the gong rang, and Nahama snatched her baby up out of his crib, but Rivka, the ruler of the infants' house, protested vigorously, out of habit, against parents coming to the cribs at all hours. Still arguing, they ran out together to greet the arrivals.

From all corners of the settlement the comrades came running toward the truck. The builders who were putting up the walls of the new house of culture dropped their pails of cement and hurried toward the central yard; the milkers in the dairy, the carpenters in the workshop, the stablemen and the tractorists, the children in torrents from their houses, all came running in the path of the truck. White-haired Abba was prancing and dancing

30

his horse around the vehicle as if he personally had engineered the entire feat.

Chayim roared through the gate, the momentum carrying the old truck triumphantly up the hill in high speed. He passed the stables and barns and circled the big yard, bringing the vehicle to a stand precisely at the entrance to the dining-hall.

Above the noise of the exultant motor the immigrants were singing, and the flying wake of settlers took up their song:

> "*Am Yisroel chai! Am Yisroel chai!*
> The nation Israel lives! The people Israel lives!"

From the back of the truck the illegals began to tumble out into the arms of the settlers.

And out of the mass of welcoming settlers the names of Europe rose.

"Budapest? Is there anyone from Budapest?"

"Frankfort?"

"From Dessau?"

"From Kovno?" Mother Zipporah was asking. "I had my sisters—"

"From Königsberg?"

"Dresden?"

"Warsaw?"

"Lodz?"

The names of towns and cities and villages, in Poland, Hungary, Czechoslovakia, the names of places in Germany and in Austria, echoed back and forth from the settlers to the immigrants, from the immigrants to the settlers, and once, and then again, it happened that two startled voices repeated the same name.

"Vilno?"

"Vilno!"

"The Ledermans?"

"I knew them well!"

"What became—" And then the silence.

David listened excitedly, expecting any moment to hear his own name called, or the name of his city. He looked at all the faces around him; it could not be like this that he would find his family. Somehow he had not thought that they would be in a big

31

place, with so many other people; it would be a little house, with trees. And yet he could not turn away from a possible moment, even here.

Marta stood near him, and she was not looking at anyone, or asking anyone. She was only waiting. David felt a mounting agony, as if surely something must happen; he had arrived, he was here in the daylight, surely someone must see him and know him, the Halevis' boy, from Cracow.

And then he saw how such a thing happened, not to him, but to young Dvora. A woman came closer and closer and stared at Dvora. She was a strong woman, a mother, with round arms, and she was carrying a baby, and an excited little girl was holding her hand. David watched as the woman studied Dvora's face. "From Bratislava?" she asked. "The Brody family?"

They were standing right next to him. The woman was not old enough to be a mother for Dvora. But the same look was coming over both their faces, breaking over everything, as though in an instant there would be a lightning that would melt them together, and David felt a panic in himself of anger and jealousy and love until he almost had to cry.

Young Dvora looked into the woman's warm eyes, and remembered Bratislava, and the little walk to the door of her house, where one lingered, parting from friends on the way home from school, and her big sister Anya's best friend, who had come so often to the house, and who once had put up Anya's long braids in a circlet around her head.

Dvora tried that girl's name. "Nahama? Nahama Beilin?"

Nahama was hugging her. Nahama was saying she looked exactly like her sister Anya had looked, those many years ago. "That's how I recognized you, Dvoraleh!"

Meanwhile Zev, the slow-spoken, tall Palestinian who had been on the truck, had made his way through the crowd to Nahama, and the little girl jumped and climbed on him devouringly, crying, "Papa! You didn't get hurt!"

This was her husband, Nahama said, her name was Nahama Feldheim now, "And these are our children, born here!"

And in that instant young Dvora had to suppress a shiver of hatred, for her sister's friend was standing here, alive, married, with children issued from her.

32

They all looked at the children, born of this place, and just then David saw how the baby wanted to go to its father, and Zev took it up on his arm, and the baby tangled his fist in Zev's black curly hair. The baby was laughing.

"And Anya?" the woman was asking Dvora.

Everyone's eyes turned to Dvora again. Stepan and Swobodniak and Ziona and all the young immigrants and the older refugees, too, David felt, were like himself, watching Dvora as if to prove through her that this miracle could happen and that people could be found again.

"Anya?" Dvora shook her head, but then quickly, as though she would not fail them all, she spoke of her brother Shlomo. "He escaped before the raids. He said he would go to Palestine. Has anyone heard of him? Shlomo Brody?"

The name passed among all the settlers.

David could scarcely breathe, for this must not fail. And from the edge of the crowd the name was echoed. The leader of the mission, Avram, caught the name and repeated it. "Shlomo Brody? But I know him! He was in the Brigade with me!"

"He's alive!" Dvora cried.

The word bounded through the whole group. "Alive! The girl's brother is alive! Avram knows him! Alive! Young Dvora's brother!"

"You can write to him, I'll give you the address," Avram said. "He's not demobilized yet."

And they beamed upon Dvora, as if she had done this thing for all of them. Her face was still dazed, and she clung to her friend, her dead sister's friend Nahama, from whom all this had come. Nahama was the proof that this was real.

Giant Stepan put his arm around Dvora. "You're a lucky one, Dvoraleh! Half a family already!"

And then David felt it was wrong, a mistake! How could this be happening to Dvora, when it was he, David, who had come to find his family! He burst out in front of all of them, the people of the settlement, all of them. "I have my whole family!" he declared. "They are here in Palestine. My father, and my mother, and I have a big brother, and a little brother, and—"

They were all looking at him and smiling; then they looked

above him, at Marta, and they looked again at him, but smiled a little differently.

Avram was writing out the address for Dvora, and the others turned away from her now. The sudden gladness was gone, and it was almost as though she had done something against all of her friends.

"I don't know their address exactly," David ended.

"Eat! Eat, children! Come, everybody, eat!" Abba called, and the Palestinians led the way into the large white building that was the dining-hall.

Lazar and Giant Stepan moved forward, but Blaustein hesitated. "Can we go in too?" he asked, to make sure. Laughing, Stepan gave him a shove.

But Nahama, hugging Dvora, had felt her wet clothes, and now she saw that many of the others were soaked. Ziona had torn her skirt in jumping out of the boat and was holding it together in her hand. "Look at the boy's shoes!" Nahama said, for the knotted strings on them had broken, and the old shoes were falling apart. "You had better come along with me and get some dry clothes before you eat." The girls all followed her, and Avram came with David.

They went into another building. Inside, the walls were lined with shelves divided into cubicles and filled from floor to ceiling with clothes. There was a special odor in the room, warm, and stinging a little, and a woman was standing there ironing. Like a mother ironing at home.

Avram made David sit down and pull off his shoes. The strings had rotted, and the bottom of one shoe was flapping. Avram handed him a pair of sandals, and some underwear, and a pair of shorts and a shirt.

Sara, who was responsible for the storeroom, left off her ironing to help Nahama with the girls. Some of the girls wore discarded soldiers' shirts, and all their clothes were patched and torn again. They had lain in these clothes for weeks.

There were cotton print dresses in the stores, and as Sara handed them out, the young girls uttered little cries, and caressed the cloth, and touched the buttons and the bits of trimming.

"New!" They could not seem to believe it. "New!" They held

34

the dresses against their bodies and could not stop feeling the cloth. "New!"

But when Nahama handed Marta a dress, the young woman felt it for a moment, fingering the bright cloth and the little tie-ribbons on the short puffed sleeves. Then suddenly she handed back the garment. "I'll keep my own," she said. "It will do."

She was wearing a long-sleeved plain brown dress, crumpled and still damp. Nahama wondered if the girl was refusing the new dress because it was light and colorful. And then a strange idea came to her. Perhaps the woman was still under the habit of the camps, still carrying a fear that she would be given one garment, only to have all of her own things taken away.

"But of course you keep your own things," Nahama said. "You'll need new clothes too."

Marta did not respond. She felt that everyone was watching her. Avram was standing there with David, and watching her, and the child was taking notice, because of Avram. It would have been better if she had simply taken the dress and said nothing. Now she could not respond, and in her panic she had fallen into her old habit of squeezing her right wrist tightly.

Suddenly there was a movement from young Dvora, who was offering to exchange new dresses with her. "Try this one," Dvora said, "I think it will suit you better, Marta."

She saw how Dvora ran her hand all the way down the long sleeve of the dress she was offering. "Thank you," Marta said. She took the garment, feeling that she had completely lost control and had done the worst thing of all. For now surely they had all noticed, even the man Avram had noticed, about the sleeves.

The other girls, Ziona, and the French girl Tessa, with their bare branded arms were like the boys, hiding nothing. And young Dvora, who did not even have numbers on her arm, felt compelled to explain herself. "I was in a nunnery the whole time," she said. "They hid me. Wasn't I lucky?"

"Come, let's try on your new clothes," Nahama said too cheerfully, and Marta followed after the others, trying to tell herself that it was time to make an end of hiding, that surely everything about her was known, and yet clutching the long-sleeved garment and realizing that in dressing she would manage to turn away from the others until she had it on.

35

Avram and David watched the women going to change their clothes, and Avram made a joke about women—even in a settlement, he said, they were fussy about their clothes. "But men have to eat!" and he clapped his hand on the back of David's neck as they walked out. "Were you with Marta all the time, in the camps?" Avram asked the boy. "No," the boy said. "Only on the ship, and just before."

The dining-hall was so large, David saw, that everyone had a place to sit. There were two long rows of tables, and windows all around, and there was a piano at the far end. At all the tables everybody was eating hard and big. Carts laden with food were being pushed along the aisles, and the tables were covered with bowls and plates filled with food. Big loaves of bread, big pots of porridge, big bowls of tomatoes and green peppers and radishes, whole plates of butter, were on every table, and in front of each person there was a dish with a whole egg. There were more eggs on the tables, in bowls, and there were dishes of olives, pitchers of milk, big pots of coffee, piles of oranges, saucers of jam— everything anyone wanted to eat was here!

Stepan made room for David at the table where all of them were together, Lazar and Swobodniak and Weisbrod. David squeezed in next to Stepan, on the bench, and looked at all the good things to eat and didn't know where to begin. But among all those things it was the bread that drew him, the big rough-cut slabs of bread, and as he held a chunk in his hand it still felt faintly warm and gave over the table the sweet odor of baking.

The old man, Abba, was walking around all the tables, telling everybody, "Eat! Eat!" And Lazar, his face all shining, his red beard shining, held up a whole bread that he was slicing. "From your own ovens?" he asked.

"From our own ovens!" Giant Stepan cried, as one who knew everything already. "Even the wheat is from our own fields!"

"Eat! Eat!" and the old man laughed.

David buttered his bread, thickly, without stint, and was almost ready to take his first bite when Stepan seized his hand. "Wait!" the Giant cried. He took a spoon, scooped a slow yellow liquid from a dish, and let it flow over the butter on David's bread. "Honey!" he proclaimed. "Our own honey! From our own bees!"

As David tasted the whole, like a melting wonder in his mouth, they poured milk for him, and Lazar again asked his question, "From our own cows?"

The solemn Zev Feldheim smiled down over the table, as though they were all children. "Everything, comrades," he said, "the milk, the honey, everything, just as it says in the Torah. It flows!"

David wondered, could it be true? Every single thing on the table, even the sugar, even the salt? Then people could live in this place without having to go out to get anything from anyone!

But Lazar had to ask again. He picked up the dish of olives. "From our own trees?"

"Of course! The product of our land!" Stepan assured him.

Stepan himself was eating with both hands, and was passing things to everyone, just as after a raid, when you have to stuff down everything because you cannot carry it away. He looked at Weisbrod, who was sitting motionless, having finished the egg on his plate. "Take more! Take more!" Stepan heaped Weisbrod's plate with tomatoes, eggs, greens. "Here it's all right to take all you want!"

Two girls were changing the empty vegetable bowls for full ones, and Abba put his arms around them, holding them near the table. "Here also is a product of our land!" he said. He called them by a Hebrew word, *sabras*. "You know what that means?" Abba said. "It is the name of the cactus that grows in Palestine— sharp outside and sweet within."

One of the girls was dark, like an Arab. Abba said her name was Bathsheba, and she was a daughter of Jews from Yemen. David wondered whether he would be so dark if he were born in Palestine.

They kept on eating, and Abba kept on talking. This was their home, he said. They were all needed in Palestine, all, there was work for everyone, builders were needed, and cobblers, machinists, electricians, farm workers, and teachers. Here in the settlement, he said, they would learn to speak Hebrew; those who already spoke a little would learn more. And they could remain, and find their places, and be at home.

Perhaps some of them would want, rather, to work in the city. "Very well," he said, "with our blessing." And some of them

37

might want to try their way in other *kibbutzim,* in other settlements, or as private farmers. "Good, with our blessing." But first
they should rest a few days. And then, if they wished, a group of
them could go out together to see the land of Palestine. "The
lucky ones," he said, "have relatives to find—"

David heard, and looked up at the old man, yes, he was like a
grandfather, with his shining circle of stiff white hair, he was
good, he was full of understanding.

David could eat no more, yet there were still things on the table.
The bread was unfinished, and there were still eggs in the bowls,
and tomatoes and radishes. Surely, even here, people did not eat
all they wanted every day. And besides, it would be well to begin
to save up food for the time when they would go out on the road.

He looked toward Stepan, and saw how Stepan reached, and
took two eggs and put them in his pocket, and took the whole
uncut end of the bread in his huge hand. And Swobodniak also,
when he thought no one was watching, hastily pocketed an egg.

But David saw that Avram had noticed everything; Avram
only smiled. So David reached, in plain sight, and took two big
slices of bread to put in his pocket.

And now since they had not slept all night, Abba said, they
should get some sleep.

In the secretariat Zipporah and Hillel were bent over the hous-
ing chart of the settlement.

"Where will we put them all? There are twice as many as we
were told," Zipporah worried.

"Well," Hillel shrugged, "do you want to send them away?"

"But where will we put them?"

Abba stuck his head into the little office. "We'll move into tents
ourselves," he suggested.

"Who? The youth group is already in tents," Zipporah reminded him.

"We old ones."

"And your malaria?" she demanded.

Abba whistled away his malaria. "It will be romantic—real
pioneers!" he jested. "In tents."

"In your grave you'll be a real pioneer," she scolded. "There on
the hill we have a place for you to lie."

"For today, while people are working," Hillel suggested, "they can rest in our beds. By tonight we will think of something. We'll arrange ourselves."

"But there aren't enough cots. Even if people move into tents, are they to lie on the ground?" Zipporah persisted.

"Very well! Then we'll send Chayim to Afikim to borrow some cots!" Hillel snapped, as if she had attacked his efficiency.

There were rows of white houses, and in each house there were four sleeping rooms. The newcomers were placed three in a room.

The beds had covers on them, and the rooms belonged to others, for there were clothes about. Avram told them this was only for now, so that they might get some rest right away; by evening they would have their own beds.

David guessed it was Avram's own bed that was given to him. Lying down, he kept thinking about what Abba had said: they could go and look for their relatives. He did not need to rest a few days, he would be ready to go at once. He wanted to wake Stepan so they could make plans, but he felt a new hesitation about Stepan. Perhaps the Giant would be angry if he woke him; and David had an uneasy feeling that Stepan might not even want to go right away from this place. Whom would he ask then? David thought of Lazar, but Lazar would do only what Stepan did. Maybe all of them would come, Stepan and young Dvora and Lazar; they could say it was only to see the country, but secretly he and Stepan would be searching for his family. Stepan would be the only one who knew the real secret, and one day they would come to the place and all the others would be surprised, and his father and mother would invite all of his friends to a wonderful feast. Perhaps tomorrow he would start on his search. He would not tell Marta he was going.

David couldn't sleep. He went out into the yard to wait for Stepan.

On the grass by the big dining-house Weisbrod lay in a reclining chair. The girl from the beach, Yehudith, was sitting with him and feeding him something from a spoon.

"What is it? Medicine?" David asked.

She laughed and asked if he wanted to taste it.

He didn't want to taste any medicine.

But it was only honey, she said. It would give him strength, and for Weisbrod, it would stop his mouth from bleeding all the time. She offered a spoonful to David, and he didn't know whether to believe her. It looked the same as the dining-room honey, but it was in a medicine bottle. Surely it was just some sour medicine.

Finally he tasted the tip of the spoon. It was honey. Yehudith was laughing at him and saying, "Why didn't you believe me?"

He didn't know what to say. But perhaps this was only a way to make him believe things, and then later on there would be something that was not true.

After a while Stepan came out with the others, Dvora and Ziona and Tessa and the bearded Lazar. The girls were already going about like the women of the settlement, with their legs bare, in shorts, as though ready to work.

David did not want to talk to all of them together; it would be better to talk to Stepan alone, first. But Stepan said they were all going around to see the farm.

"Do you think we can go by ourselves? Shouldn't we ask someone where we can go?" Tessa worried, but Stepan laughed at her. "We can go anywhere," he said.

"Yes," David reminded them all, "the old grandfather, Abba, said we could even go away from here if we wanted."

David was not eager to look at the farm; he would see a wonderful farm when he came to his father's house. But he walked along with them, so as to get a chance to talk to Stepan.

They went through rows of plants, and Stepan showed him tomatoes growing. Stepan and Lazar pulled the pale green tomatoes from the stems, and walked along, eating them. "Good! Better than fruit!" Stepan said. And he already knew about this settlement, that it grew the biggest and the earliest tomatoes in all Palestine. They went through a vineyard, and though it was not the time for grapes, Stepan assured them that the vines were strong and excellently tended. And they went through a lemon grove, and an orange grove, and pulled fruit from the trees, and Stepan and Dvora began to sing one of the Hebrew songs they had learned in the camp after the liberation.

David was thinking how it would be with his family. Would he speak Polish to them at home, or would they be speaking Hebrew, now that they lived in Palestine? They would be surprised that he was grown so big, and at all the Hebrew he had learned in the camp.

They passed among tall palm trees, and Stepan told Dvora that there was even fruit growing high up in these trees, dates, which they had never tasted and which were very sweet; and later in the year they would taste this fruit. Then they came to a grove of smaller trees with whole bunches of bananas within reach.

"Everything grows here in Palestine," David said, walking along beside Stepan. "It would be easy to live on the road."

Dvora was walking on the other side of Stepan, and she wanted to pick some bananas, but Stepan told her one of the comrades had warned him that you could not eat bananas right off the trees, they would make you sick, you had to let them dry for a week. Lazar said, "Hah! That is only to keep us from picking them." But Stepan said it was true, he was certain. Sometimes David wondered where his big friend had learned everything; and again he felt all dark inside at the thought of trying to go on the road without Stepan.

"It would be easier on the road here than in Europe," David said, not caring any more who heard, for young Dvora stayed close to Stepan all the time now. "Stepan, we could go and find my family." He saw exactly how his family would be living, in a white house with a red roof, and with banana trees and apple and plum trees in the yard, and a whole yard filled with hens running about and clucking and eating bread crumbs because there was so much bread, and laying eggs everywhere. "You could stay and live with us," he said to Stepan. "We have everything in our house."

Dvora said, "But we have everything right here, David!" She gave Stepan half an orange she had peeled.

Just then Ziona made a terrible noise, spitting out part of a banana, and laughing at herself, because she had not believed about the bananas and had picked and eaten one. And Dvora said, "You see! Stepan was right!"

They came out of the grove to a large field, where people were working. There were long rows of young green shoots, and the settlers were spread out among the rows, hoeing. Stepan said this was maize. Zev and Abba were already at work here, and several of the girls from the colony were also in the group. They cried out *shalom!* to the newcomers, and asked how they liked the farm, and asked the question that David knew already everyone would ask over and over—how did it feel to be home at last?

Stepan bent down and took a handful of earth and rubbed it in his fingers, like an expert. "Good soil!" he pronounced, and Abba chuckled at him. Abba stopped working and took a drink from a jug, holding it above his mouth and letting the water spout down into his throat.

"Once this was a swamp," he informed them. "Swamps make good soil."

Stepan stood there staring at the people swinging their mattocks and hoes, and all the others stared too, as though this were something wonderful. Suddenly Stepan walked into the field and reached his hand out for a hoe. "Give me one of those!" he said.

Zev straightened up and looked at Stepan with his small smile, as if he knew everything about everybody. "You'll have enough work in your life, comrade," he said. "You know what it says in the Torah—'the earth abideth forever.' So she can wait a little longer for your hands."

Everyone laughed, but Abba tossed his mattock to Stepan, and it was like a twig in his giant hands. He bent and began to chop the earth, and they laughed and made jokes at his fervor. "You're not digging to China," they told him. "It's only weeds!"

But Lazar, too, had to start to work at once, and Dvora took a hoe from a pile on the ground, and soon they were mixed in among the others, and David saw that in the clothes they had been given this morning it was not easy to tell his companions from the people of the place.

"You know what we'll do, Dvoraleh," Stepan said, swinging his mattock as he talked, chopping the ground with each breath, "we'll ask for new land—hnnh! And horses and machinery—hnnh! And we'll plow—*hnnh!*" He bent over and pulled at a long trailing weed whose roots stretched far under the ground, and Abba taught him its name, *yablit,* and said this weed was the greatest enemy of the settlements, worse even than the British, and Stepan and Dvora knelt and pursued it into the earth with their hands, as if indeed they were tracking a foe.

Then David knew that his plan was lost, but he could not quite believe it had happened so quickly and finally with his friend of all the camps and all the roads. He advanced a little toward

Stepan and reminded him, "Abba said we could go first and see all of Palestine and look for our relatives."

But Stepan only smiled, as at a child's distraction. "Maybe sometime we will," he said, and went on working.

After a few hours of sleep Avram had a session with Zipporah in the secretariat. She was still complaining that the settlement couldn't take such a burden. Even to feed the newcomers, there simply wasn't enough capacity in the pots, in the kitchen; and the budget, and clothes—

"Well, Akiba had a fishing boat, so he packed them in like fish," Avram said. "He had four hundred instead of two hundred. We each have to double our load."

"There aren't enough mosquito nets," she complained. "They'll all get sick on us. Why didn't someone think of that when the truck went for cots?"

"It can't go back again today," he said. "But if they have no nets for one night, they won't complain. And why do you have to think of them as a burden, as the sickly dregs of Europe? They're just what we need," Avram declared. "Young and tough. Didn't you look at them?"

Most of them, Avram thought, as he left, most of them would be no trouble. Hebrew classes would have to be organized right away. It was always best to give them an immediate feeling of concern for them, and action. A few of the problem ones he recognized already.

For the typical problems he was prepared. The suspicion that was deep in their blood now, nothing could be done for that, except that they would have to live it out, and in time it would diminish in most of them. Even the collapsed ones, like Weisbrod, might partly mend in time.

The matter of the child came into his mind again. Perhaps the best thing would be to try to bind him to a family, to the Feldheims, for instance. Or should the boy remain for the time being with his little group? Would it be better to have him sleep in a room with his companions from Europe, or in the children's house? And Avram wondered if by any freak of destiny the child's parents could really be alive.

As he was passing the old cabin that had been fixed up as a

reading-room and library, Avram glanced in at the window and recognized the dark young woman, Marta. She was moving slowly along the wall of books, touching the volumes with her hands. He could have guessed she was an intellectual.

She was another one who would be difficult, mostly because she would try to do it all for herself. In some way, Avram realized, the woman was linked to the boy, and in this he would have to be careful. It might be better for her and the boy to develop that bond, rather than let the boy attach himself to a family of the settlement, like the Feldheims. He would have to discuss this with Zev and Nahama, for who was he, a childless comrade, to make such decisions.

Avram wondered whether he should go into the library and try to talk to the young woman. She, too, would be part of his task. As he entered, Avram noticed that she began to replace the book she held in her hand, but then checked herself and faced him.

"Good to see books again?" Avram said.

She replied impersonally, "Yes."

He always felt constrained by intellectuals. "I see you would rather read than sleep," he remarked.

"I slept a little," she said.

He noticed that the book in her hand was from the psychology shelf. That was the favorite reading of Hillel, the secretary, he remarked. Avram had listened to a few of Hillel's lectures, in the cultural evenings that Zev was always organizing, and he knew the general names that everyone knew; he had even glanced at some of the Hebrew translations of Freud, Jung, and Adler on these shelves. There were other volumes in German and English—Ferenzi, Stekel.

"You have all of them," she said, and he was proud of her surprise, for it was always a little amusing to have visitors and newcomers surprised to find books in a settlement.

"We don't have them all translated into Hebrew yet," he said, "and the ones in English I read too slowly. You are a student?" he ventured. He had almost said "were."

"No," she said. She put the book away.

It was difficult to go on with her. "We don't all read as much as we should," Avram said. "I always have plans to read, but then

44

I always have something else to do. Still, some of the comrades keep up their reading. Hillel—the one with the glasses—he is always reading; you will find him here whenever he's free. And Zev Feldheim you know already, he was with us on the truck. He is our scholar, in charge of this library. If there is anything special you want, ask Zev, and he will get it for you from the settlement libraries."

"There is nothing I want," she said.

Her manner was so final that Avram nearly replied, "You mean nothing should be wanted of you." The only way to reach her would be through the boy—if there was still a way to reach her at all. Well, she was grown, she could be responsible for herself if she so insisted. "The boy," he said, "I suppose that is just an idea of his, about his family?"

"Yes. As you see."

"Do you—is anything known about his family?"

"No," she said. "Like the others."

He wanted to ask her about herself, but she left no way open. "Perhaps he will give it up as he gets involved in the life here."

"He has to give it up," she said.

It was strange, how cold she seemed in talking of it, and yet he had noticed how she was with the boy, always near him, within reach.

Chapter Three

That evening after supper Avram waited for the usual little groups to form around the tables, and he saw that many of the newcomers were lingering. Most of them still clung together, but here and there one could be seen talking to the comrades of Makor Gallil.

Avram pulled a chair over to the end of the table where several of the young refugees were congregated—Stepan and his cohorts.

They were plaguing Lazar about shaving off his beard. David was with them, and Marta, as Avram had expected, was sitting with the boy. Avram poured himself a mug of tea. He made a joke about Stepan's already famous eagerness to get to work on his first day, and Stepan twisted his huge hands, grinning self-consciously.

"Where should I work tomorrow?" Stepan asked. "Can I learn how to plow? With horses?"

"No, with a tractor!" the girl Ziona cried.

Abba leaned over from the next table, where he was sitting with Weisbrod. "You have other things to learn besides work, children," he reminded them.

Yes, they wanted to study too, they agreed; they wanted to learn everything, they knew nothing. Ziona declared she had once known how to write Polish but had forgotten, for even if writing had been permitted, she had no one left to write to. But that didn't matter. What was Polish! She would start anew, with Hebrew. The French girl wanted to learn nursing, and Lazar wanted to become an expert.

"An expert of what?" Avram asked.

"Anything," the red-beard said dreamily. "A mechanic, or to raise cows. I don't know. But an expert."

Zev and Nahama came along and sat down at the table with them, and several more of the refugees joined the little circle until the two tables made a warm lively group.

Each of them would become an expert, a specialist, Stepan declared, and then they would go on their own land, to build their own settlement.

"So fast?" Abba said.

Yehudith and Amos smiled at the innocence of the newcomers. "Wait, wait, friends," Yehudith said, "in Eretz Yisroel you learn how to wait. Our youth group has been waiting two years for land for our own settlement."

Weisbrod, sitting there, had the lost melancholy look of one who feels himself out of place, and yet is so much in need of being among people that he cannot take himself away from their warmth.

"And you?" Abba said to Weisbrod. "You too, want to go start a new settlement?"

46

Weisbrod mumbled his answer. He wouldn't be any use for anything. There was nothing he could do. As a young man, yes, he had always had a dream, to go onto the land, to be a farmer, that was after all the best thing. He had been strong, then, an amateur gymnast—could they imagine it?

No one denied him, for it was indeed impossible to imagine, to clothe his skeletal form with muscles. But then he fell silent, as though he had broken a code he kept with himself: a man did not talk of what had been.

"You are from a city then?" Abba asked.

"From Breslau."

"You had a family?"

"A wife and two children."

"What did you do, then, in Breslau?"

Weisbrod's whisper was barely audible. "A physician."

Avram caught and checked himself before he brought out the remark that would naturally have followed, that doctors were always needed, that there was even a gradual reapprenticeship for doctors from Europe, through the Sick Fund, the Kupat Cholim. For he saw that Weisbrod was shaking his head, without forcefulness, but with a finality, a recognition of something dead.

"No, no, nothing to do with that. Not any more." His bony nervous hands had been lying on the table; now he dropped them into his lap, as though to keep them out of his own sight. "I always believed," Weisbrod resumed in his lost whisper, "a man should know how to live on the land. But we—we never learned how to live."

"How could we?" Abba declared. "In my day in old Russia a Jew was even forbidden to buy land. So we were all shopkeepers, lawyers, doctors."

"And sweatshop workers," Zipporah put in.

Weisbrod's eyes remained fixed on the table.

"It's not too late!" Abba seemed to be forcing his own energy into the man. "You're not too old! Look at me! I am as good as any of these sprouts! A man of fifty is worth two of twenty-five! And you're surely no older than I am! Are you past fifty?"

Avram wished his father had not spoken. For with scarcely a movement of his lips Weisbrod replied, "No, I am not yet past fifty. I am thirty-four."

Hastily Zipporah tried to dispel the embarrassment. "More tea! Have more tea!" she insisted.

But Abba rode over it loudly. Perhaps that was the best way. "Thirty-four!" he bellowed. "And he is trying to act like an old man! You have a whole new life! And for a new life," he declared, "you need a new name. Jaroslav! Is that a name for a Palestinian?"

"Jeremiah," Zipporah suggested, "because he is a pessimist, a worrier, like me. Call him Jeremiah."

They all laughed, and a wan, bitter smile appeared on Weisbrod's face. He drank his tea.

Abba turned on Stepan. "You, too! Stepan! Is that a name for a Jew? A boy who wants to plow the fields of Israel with his very fingers!"

"Well, it was a good name for Poland," Stepan explained, "because that was how I remained alive. They took me for a Pole. My father was a contractor in Warsaw. It wasn't even so Jewish, in our house. We lived among the Poles. So there was one, a carpenter, who took me to live with him."

"He knew?"

"He knew. He was a good one."

"But still they caught you."

"No," Stepan said. "The whole time I lived outside the ghetto. I didn't go into the ghetto until the last."

Zev Feldheim, sitting next to Stepan, caught the remark. "You were outside the ghetto and went back in?" he asked.

"Well, yes," Stepan said. "They were fighting."

And after the end of the ghetto he and two others had found themselves alive. They had gone into the woods, among the partisans. From there the story was like others Avram had heard, the strange chain of miracles interrupted by bad luck, and again miracles of survival. One day, going into a village for food, Stepan had been caught in a chance round-up. Fortunately he was not taken to be destroyed as a Jew, but mixed among a group of Poles. He had been transported to a labor camp, and from there, and from there—

It was like telling of the army, Avram knew; the things that could never be communicated you summed up in a line— "We went from here to there." And that was why you held together,

48

afterward, with those who had gone the same journey. And that was why it might be best for them to remain together.

"Stepan!" Abba repeated, and the boy grinned back self-consciously, looking exactly like a young Polish peasant. "What can we name him?"

They tried out names for him. Shimon, that sounded close to Stepan. And Zev had a suggestion that he be called Oved, the worker.

Then Stepan himself asked, "Isn't there a name, like after a fighter? A Jewish fighter?"

Surely, Avram thought, they should have come to that themselves. "Why not let him be called Maccabee?" he said.

"Maccabee?" Stepan repeated. "Who was that?"

The Palestinians glanced at one another. And yet he had been a Jewish child. "The Maccabees were a family of soldiers," Avram explained. "Partisans. They fought against the Greeks when our people were conquered, here in our land."

Lazar had brought to the table a folded and creased map of Palestine that he had carried in his pocket all these months. Zev reached for it and traced with his finger the battles of the Maccabees, showing how they had driven out the Greeks. "They even fought here, in the hills of Naphtali, behind us," he said. "You can see the caves where they had their strongholds."

The name was a good choice for Stepan. He was pleased. "David," he said, "try my new name." He wanted to hear it from a familiar voice.

"Maccabee," the boy said, but he spoke the name softly, Avram noticed, as though merely in obedience, and against his own inclination. David had taken the map of Palestine and was staring at it now, with his finger on the spot Lazar had already marked, where the colony stood.

Awkwardly the newly named Maccabee was telling how he wanted to learn all about history, and about the way the world was formed, about the Jordan River and how it cut its way down to the Dead Sea, and about the volcanic rocks that lay on the fields, and why so much of this land was dry and dead. All, all, he wanted to learn, all in one gulp. And he wanted to learn to do every-thing—to raise sheep, to raise fruit, to irrigate, to plow. "I was still

49

in school when the war started," he said, "so I never learned any job, only to carry and dig."

"And to fight," David said.

Now they all wanted to have new names, except Ziona, who was proud that she had carried her Hebrew name from birth. The bearded Lazar changed his first name from Peter to Ben-Ari, the son of a lion, and a Haddassah and a Bar Kochba were also born, and the little French girl, Tessa, became Tirza.

Only Marta had not yet spoken, and as the others told about themselves and seemed to come one by one into a newness, she seemed more and more isolated, until Avram began to fear that she would rise and go away and remain outside of the new thing that was forming.

Then a little pause came, just after Tessa had taken the name of Tirza, and was enchantedly repeating after Zev the chain of her generations. The father of all was Joseph, whose son was Manasseh, who was the father of Machir, whose son was Gilead, father of Hepher, father of Zelophehad, and Zelophehad fathered only daughters, and Tirza was the youngest of his daughters, and because there was no son in their house, the daughters stood before Moses, and because of their plea Moses recognized the rights of women and the succession of the family through women as well as men. That was who Tirza was! And it was a good name, she said, for there were no men left in her house either.

Then they all realized that only Marta remained. Nahama turned to her. "And you?" she said.

Avram saw that the girl had been preparing herself for the moment. She recited her particulars, but it was not as the others had done, as though sending feelers out, seeking places of attachment. From her the story came by rote, in one piece, as much as to recognize that she owed an answer to the interrogation by the community and wanted to finish with her turn as briefly as possible and without contact.

"The same happened as to everyone," she said. She was from Vienna. She had had a husband and child. The husband had taught at the University of Vienna. They had been taken all together to Auschwitz. Her husband and baby had been destroyed. "I was passed as fit for use."

50

The recital was as precise as a reply to an official questioning. There seemed nothing to say to her.

"Marta," Nahama repeated, "perhaps you would like to change your name to Miriam?"

"You may change my name if you wish," she said. Avram noticed that she was clasping her wrist tightly, as she had done in the clothing-room. "A new name doesn't change anything."

Suddenly the boy David cried out, "Nobody is going to change my name!" They had changed Stepan's name, and they were even changing Marta's. Surely they would try to take away his name too, the name that his father had given him.

And as they didn't answer, David explained to them, "Suppose my mother and father came to find me. They would ask for David, and nobody would know whom they meant." He waited, ready to resist, expecting them to propose strange-sounding names, but instead the Palestinians only smiled at him.

"Why should anyone want to change such a name as David?" Abba said. "It's a fine Hebrew name. It is the name of our greatest king."

"Only with us," Zev said, "David is pronounced Daavid. Your father would be sure to recognize it just the same."

While Zev spoke, his little daughter Shulamith was climbing all over him. She settled on her father's shoulders and kept her eyes on Daavid.

"Daavid, Daavid and Goliath!" she repeated.

"I heard about David and Goliath," he said.

"Who told you the story? Your father?" Avram asked.

"Yes," he declared, "my father. He told me all kinds of wonderful stories. Every night."

But then Miriam looked directly into his eyes, and he knew what she meant, for it was she who had told him the story of David and Goliath, one time, on the boat.

The little girl's mother, Nahama, asked him if he remembered how his father looked. "Was he a tall man?" she asked.

How could he not remember! "My father is tall!" Daavid told them. "And he said I would be even taller."

"As tall as Avram?" the little girl's mother asked.

Daavid was not sure exactly how tall, because he himself had

51

been much littler then, and he had had to look straight up to see his father. But he replied, "Taller."

Miriam said, "Every five-year-old's father seems tall."

Then there were more questions about his father. Abba asked, "Did he have a beard?"

Sometimes it seemed to Daavid that his father had a strong, dark short beard. Or was that his grandfather? And sometimes he thought of his father with only a mustache. "I think he has a black mustache," Daavid said.

Then Zev asked, "What kind of work did he do?" And Nahama asked, "Did he carry a little black bag, like a doctor? Did he have a shop?"

Whenever Daavid looked at big machines, at bridges and trains, he always thought, my father can build things like that. He told them his father was a big man, who did big works. "He went to work every day," he said, "and every night he came home."

He had told all these things before to Marta, who was now Miriam. Many times he had told her all he knew about his family, and each time when she listened and he told her more things than before, it was as though she were holding them for him. Some of these things he seemed to be drawing back from her now, and he told the others these things, how there was singing in the house, and his father played the violin.

"Was he a musician then?" they asked.

"In the evening, at home, he played, and everybody sang," Daavid said.

Then Abba asked him, "What was your father's name, Daavid?"

"His name?" Daavid repeated. "His name is papa."

The little girl laughed. Her mother gave her a reproving look, and Daavid knew she was just a child and didn't understand anything.

"Papa is what you called him," Nahama said. "But what did other people call him?"

"They call him Halevi—our name," he replied.

"What did your mother call him?" Avram asked.

Daavid easily remembered. "She calls him 'dearest.'"

"He was too young to remember everything very clearly," Miriam said.

52

Why did she have to say things like that? "Yes, I remember!" Daavid declared. And he told them all the things in a rush of words. "My father—he can fix anything. When my wagon broke, he made a new axle, and when anything broke in the house, my mother asked him, and he fixed it. He had all kinds of tools. My brother could use them, but I was too young, but now I am old enough and he would let me use everything, even the saws. I can use a saw already."

"We have tools in the carpentry shed," Avram told him. "If you want, ask Moshe, in the carpentry, he will show you how to use them."

"Did you have brothers and sisters?" Nahama asked Daavid.

Miriam was looking at him as though to stop him. Daavid looked away from her and said anything that came into his mind, just to show her that he remembered even more than he had ever told her. "I have a big brother," he said, "and two sisters."

"What was your brother's name?" they asked.

Maccabee offered it. "Samuel," he said. "Daavid told me."

"Yes, Samuel," Daavid said. "And I have a baby sister. I have twin baby sisters. And my mother sings to them." He looked directly at Miriam again, for she never sang.

"What was she like, your mother?" they asked.

"My mother?" Miriam did not turn her eyes away. "My mother—" he repeated.

"Did she have dark hair, like Miriam's?" Nahama asked.

"My mother has long, long hair," Daavid said. "Her name is Esther."

The little girl climbed down from her father's shoulders, and came around, close to him.

"Did they take your mother away, together with your father?" Nahama asked.

"They took us all together, to a place near a train," Daavid said. He told them how everybody was there, his big brother, all of his brothers and sisters and his grandfather, everybody, the whole family and the whole street, and as he spoke he saw them crowding until it was hard to keep in his mind the faces that were of his family, uncles, and cousins, and the faces that were friends who came to the house and were also called uncles but weren't real uncles, and he told how they all came, more and more of them into

53

the square in front of the railway station, and the soldiers were all around with machine guns, and then how his father told him to run, run in the woods, and gave him a push, and how he dodged between the legs of soldiers, and ran, and hid in the woods.

"For a long time?" the little girl Shulamith asked.

"Oh, weeks, I think," he said. "Years."

"How did you live? What did you eat?" they asked.

"I was like a robber in the woods," he told them. "I went out into the fields and sometimes I stole milk from the cows. I took all kinds of food."

"Where did you sleep, child?" Nahama asked.

"In a cave," he said. "And sometimes in the trees."

He was not sure himself any more, but if it had not been so, then how did he remember such things, in his bones?

"How did you live in the winter?" Zev asked.

"Sometimes," Daavid told them, "I would go to the farmhouses and ask for something to eat and a place to sleep."

"And were the people kind to you?"

"Sometimes, and other times they chased me away. They had dogs."

"And how long did you live this way?" Avram asked.

"Maybe two years," Daavid said thoughtfully, because winter came more than once.

"But surely you were not alone all this time?" Zev said.

"No, not all the time," he told them. But he couldn't tell them of all the ways he had been alone and not alone. The memories and the pictures that came to his mind were like a scattered pack of cards, one partly covering the other. He had memories of running away from people, from other boys especially, because they might steal your food if you had any, or your secrets, or they might sell you to the Germans. Then he remembered being with three other boys, friends, bigger boys than himself, going out and raiding a farmhouse together. Then he remembered men that were his friends, partisans, one who was named Yankle. And how he ran everywhere Yankle told him to run, because he could get into places, being small. Then he remembered dead ones, Yankle, too.

They were all looking at him; he had fallen silent. "Then I got caught," he said. "A peasant caught me when I was taking potatoes. I found where he hid his potatoes under the barn, and he

54

caught me. He took me to the Germans and they took me away."

"To Auschwitz." They knew.

They also knew that in Auschwitz children were sent to the crematorium. And Daavid saw that they wondered how he had lived, and in himself he felt the strange thing that he had sometimes felt before, like shame at being alive when you were supposed to be dead. He always answered the shame in himself by telling himself he had to live because he had still to find his family. He had to do everything to live, just as he had done when the people were being loaded on the truck for the gas chambers, and he had jumped off, and the corporal had caught him by the shoulders, and he had cried out, "I have to live, I have to live, I will do anything!" And the corporal had laughed and said, "What can you do?"

And in that moment he had said crazily, "Clean your boots, every day! I can clean your boots, four times a day even!" And the corporal was holding him by the shoulders as if to lift him and throw him back onto the truck.

"With what will you clean my boots, little Yid?"

"With my bare hands, I'll polish them."

"With your tongue, you'll polish them!"

Yes, on the ground, with his tongue.

Daavid could no longer look at any of them. And he heard Stepan—Maccabee—telling them the rest, but not all the rest. He felt between himself and Stepan the bond of things that could not be told to others. Even after what had happened today in the fields, even after the way Stepan had not wanted to go on the road with him, this was still between them, the things that they knew together, of what you did to live.

"There was a transport for Buchenwald," Maccabee said, "and we smuggled him in with us. In Buchenwald a few children were allowed to remain alive." And then after the Americans came, they had started over the roads together, to the other camps, to Bergen-Belsen, and Dachau, where Maccabee kept looking for his relatives until he decided not to look any more.

"But my family wasn't in any of the camps, my family is here in Palestine," Daavid explained to them. "When my father told me to run into the woods, he said after everything was over I would find them again in Palestine."

55

In Dachau, Maccabee related, they had heard there was a way to come to Palestine, from Italy. So they had walked together, over the Alps, and found the way.

"When can I go look for my family?" Daavid asked. "Tomorrow?"

The little girl was leaning over his arm. She studied his numbers and touched them with her finger. "Is that so you wouldn't get lost from each other on the way?" she said.

"No," Daavid said, "it's my number."

Her mother explained to her, "In a place where they were slaves, Shulamith, bad people took away their names and put numbers on their arms instead of names."

"Is that why we are giving them new names?" the little girl asked.

"Yes," her father said. He picked her up and swung her up on his shoulders, to take her to bed. Daavid watched the child riding on her tall father's shoulders. He himself was too big for that kind of thing now. He could almost remember what it was like.

Miriam rose too, for she wanted to make sure that a place had been arranged for Daavid. "Do you know where Daavid is to sleep tonight?" she asked Nahama. "I think he was just using Avram's bed this afternoon."

Avram also rose. It was still a question, Avram said, whether or not to put Daavid in the children's house. "I thought of putting him in a room with his friends for a little while, until he gets used to everything here. He could remain with Maccabee and Lazar."

"Why shouldn't he live with the other children?" Miriam asked.

This was the point he wanted to discuss, Avram said. Actually Daavid was somewhat older than the oldest group of *kibbutz* children. His schooling would not present so much of a problem, since he had missed schooling entirely and would have to begin in the early grades. But for the first days, Avram had thought, it might be easier for Daavid to adjust himself if he remained with his comrades.

"But why confuse him?" Miriam said. "He is a child, and as the other children are together, he should be with them."

Avram looked to Nahama. She was in agreement with Miriam.

56

"It's best for him to realize from the beginning that he has a new kind of life here. And it is none too soon," Nahama added, "for the boy to begin to feel what it is like to be a child."

Daavid took his things from Avram's room and went with Avram and Miriam to the children's house. They entered a room filled with children and toys. The chairs and tables were small-size, especially built for the children—almost like toys. There were some fathers and mothers there, and the dark grown-up girl from Yemen, Bathsheba, was sitting among a circle of boys and girls, and they were singing.

"This was our first crop," Avram said to Miriam. "It was a good season—for our first year on the place."

Nahama was there, kneeling in front of Shulamith and helping her button her pajamas. Avram asked Nahama how many of the children were already eight years old.

"Nineteen," she said.

Though Daavid was three years older, several of the boys were as big as he. They had blocks on the floor and were building a fort. Shulamith said it was like the Maccabees against the Greeks, but a red-headed boy said no, it was against the English. This boy's father, who was also red-headed, was sitting on the floor, helping in the job.

There was a mother reading from a picture-book, with two children close against her sides, and another mother was combing a girl's hair.

Almost all the children were already in their pajamas. Across the hallway was a bathroom with washbowls and everything small, for children, and some of them were walking in and out, brushing their teeth.

Nahama told the children that Daavid was coming to live with them and said that Miriam was a new aunt.

They looked at her and said, *"Shalom,* Aunt Miriam." And Shulamith came close, as if she were already someone special to Miriam and Daavid. Then some of the other girls came near, and even some little boys, as if they wanted to feel what the new aunt was like.

"In our settlements," Nahama said to Miriam, "all grownups are aunts and uncles."

"Is this aunt a mother, too?" one of the little girls asked, and Daavid knew they were all putting Miriam together with him.

Shulamith took Miriam's hand and rubbed her face against it, and said, "Aunt Miriam, can't you be Daavid's mother?"

Daavid saw what she was doing. Her fingers were on the edge of Miriam's sleeve, and she wanted to see if Miriam had numbers, the same as his.

Miriam pulled her hand away. "No, I'm not his mother," she said, and Daavid was proud of her. Sometimes she was the only one who knew anything.

Nahama said, "Daavid, we have your place all ready for you, in a room with two other boys—Menahem and Gideon."

Across the hall there were several rooms, and in each of them he saw three or four small beds. Along the hall were rows of hooks for clothes, and shoes in pairs were set on the floor under the clothes.

Two boys were already in his room. One of them was in bed, and his mother kissed him good night on his forehead, and said *shalom* to everybody, and left. The other boy was laughing as he wrestled with his father, who would pretend to be thrown on the bed and then would suddenly spring up and reverse the positions so that the boy was pinned down flat, and still laughing. The father's name was Ephraim; he was only a small man. The boy was Gideon; he had good muscles, and bruises on his knees.

The boy who was already in bed watched Daavid as Nahama gave him a pair of pajamas. Then she went away, leaving him with Miriam.

Miriam said, "Sleep well, Daavid," and left. She knew he was big enough and didn't need a mother to put him to bed.

Avram waited on the porch, to show Miriam the way to her place, since the houses were all of the same pattern, and she probably did not yet remember in which one she lived.

He had noticed how it was when the children flocked around her. Surely this was the way to reach her. And in walking toward the cottage where she shared a room with Dvora and Tirza, Avram purposefully chose a path that went by the half-finished walls of the next children's house. "We build one every year," he explained to her, "a new grade each year, as they grow." The scaffolding of the structure was exciting to him, against the soft night sky, and he saw that a wall was standing that had not been there yesterday. Avram stopped to move away some planks that a comrade had carelessly stacked against the year-old saplings that were struggling to establish themselves in the lane.

"Perhaps you would like to work with the children?" he suggested.

"No," she said, "I'd rather not."

Her finality startled him. "Nahama really needs help," Avram said.

"I'll work in the kitchen, or anywhere. Not with children," she declared.

She spoke too strongly, she was still struggling against the feeling of that room filled with children. Then this was the moment to press her. "But you like children!" he insisted. And in the dark it was possible to touch on things one might not say otherwise. "What if the child tried to look at your arm?" he said. "It was only natural. We here, we like our children to take things so—directly. Isn't that the best way for you too?"

For a moment he felt that he had succeeded with her. Her voice now was troubled, and human. It was surely her voice from whatever life she had had, long ago, at home. "Oh, no, I couldn't endure it, all of them, all at once, so close," she confessed. "All the children all around me."

Suddenly she stopped, as one who has involuntarily shown something personal to a stranger, mistaken in the dark for an intimate. And her other voice came back. She turned on him with a hostility that was like a revenge upon her own momentary tenderness. "And you, why did you keep on asking the boy about his family, over and over! For weeks I've been trying to break this illusion."

"Are you sure it is an illusion?" Avram said.

"What else?" she demanded. "They are dead, those of his family that ever lived, except in his imagination. Polish Jews taken six years ago are dead."

"And if it helps him to believe they are alive?" Avram persisted.

She turned on him. "You yourself just said you want your children to understand the truth!"

"Yes," Avram said. "But he—"

59

"He's different! He's a refugee. He must be treated like a sick person!"

It was true, that had been in his thought. And yet he could not feel that her harshness was justified. "He is a child," Avram said. "Perhaps he is not yet able to take things as directly as you believe you can take them." She was silent. He could not help adding, "You might even learn something from him."

Miriam looked at him stonily. "Good night," she said, and walked toward her place.

"*Shalom,* friend," Avram said.

He would have to try again, another time, after she settled down a little and began to breathe. But he had not been wrong about her feelings for children. She would be among those who hurt themselves in their perversity, denying themselves what they most wanted out of some obscure need to continue suffering.

Chapter Four

Early the next morning Daavid went out by himself to make a plan. For surely no one here would help him find his family.

Some children were playing in the yard; they ran after a haycart and climbed up on it. His roommate Gideon leaped up next to the driver, who pretended to let him drive. Shulamith jumped on the wagon too, and called to Daavid. But he went on his way.

He saw the truck standing near a shed, where people were working. This was the shop filled with tools, of which Avram had spoken. Two men, holding a long saw between them, were cutting a log. It worked by a motor.

"*Shalom,* Daavid!" one of the men called to him. "Did you ever see a saw that works by electricity?"

He had not seen it, but he did not say so to them. He stood by and watched the saw cut through the log, like a knife through bread. Perhaps some day he could hide in the truck; yes, that would be easy. He had only to wait and find out when it was going to leave.

The Arab came, the same one who had been on the road yesterday, but he was without his camels. His boy and his donkey were with him, and the donkey was loaded with long reeds, of the sort that grew by the river. In the carpentry shop Daavid saw several men and women making all sorts of furniture from the reeds.

Abba came out of the shop with a lively greeting for the Arab and helped him unload the reeds.

Daavid moved close to the donkey. It was a gray donkey, and fat. He laid his hand on the animal's neck, and then gripped its forelock, as one who knows his way with such animals. The Arab boy, Mustafa, did not look unfriendly. It was his own donkey, he said. He spoke partly in Hebrew, and it was easy to understand from his signs what he was saying.

"Do you ride him all the time?" Daavid asked. The Arab boy understood him and grinned. "Sure."

"Far?" Daavid asked, looking up toward the bare hills.

Mustafa smiled confidently. "Nazareth," he said. "I was to Nazareth all by myself." He could go all over Palestine on his donkey, he told Daavid.

Jamal and Abba carried the bundles of reeds into the little factory. They were fine long reeds, Jamal pointed out, and thick. They were from the middle of the swamp, he declared, where Jews would not go because of the fever.

Indeed they were excellent reeds, Abba responded, speaking in Arabic for his guest's honor, but he would not wish his friend Jamal to expose himself to the fever for the sake of a thicker stalk. And he hoped there was no sickness in the village from laboring in the swamp. It was a bed of death, as the Arabs had so well named it, and it was a place to be avoided.

No, Jamal said, thanks be to Allah, there was little sickness just now; and in truth there was some thought of planting rice in the swamp. He watched cleverly for the result of his words upon Abba.

Comrade Moshe Seitz, at the bandsaw, grinned and winked and spoke a few rapid words in German, for Hebrew was not safe with Jamal. The reeds grew just as tall and heavy at the bend of the Jordan, on the settlement's own shore, where Jamal had certainly cut them, Moshe suggested, but why should one deprive a good Arab of his little story? As for the rice planting—let Jamal tell his tales to the British if he wanted to make a claim on the swamp. "Your old Arab is only teasing us to bring up his price."

Jamal stood staring, fascinated as always by the electric saw, while Abba fetched a tin of gasoline in payment for several loads of reeds. Gasoline was high now, and a tin was worth two pounds. As always, Abba felt the disapproving eyes of Comrade Moshe upon him. This question had been debated many times: for Seitz maintained that it would be just as cheap, if not a little cheaper, to run the tractor and a powersaw down to the riverbank, cut the reeds by machine, and haul them to the shop by means of the tractor, thus laying in a whole season's supply at one time. But Abba always argued that there was a better use for tractors than hauling reeds up the steep embankment, and, moreover, there were good reasons for supplying Jamal with an easy livelihood.

Now, as Abba carried the gasoline tin out to where the donkey stood, he saw that Jamal was studying him with his tentative smile that meant a bargain was in preparation. "One tin will make an uneven burden," Jamal pointed out. "*Hawaja* Abba, it is always better, if you have one on one side, to have another on the other side. Thus, when things are balanced, the donkey does not notice the weight of his burden and carries it happily."

Abba shook his head over Jamal's guile. Then he resisted, in the traditional manner, in order to give Jamal the full sweetness of a triumph in bargaining. But, nevertheless, he decided to advance the Arab another tin of gasoline, for there was a certain matter to be discussed, and Jamal had himself already touched upon the subject.

As the second tin was brought, Jamal responded in the way of a man who understood his friend's motive, and he approached the main subject himself, from another direction.

"You received many new people yesterday," Jamal said. "May they thrive in their new home."

"May that be the will of your God, and ours," Abba said.

How many had come? Jamal inquired with frank curiosity. It had seemed to him yesterday morning that the springs of the truck were depressed almost flat by the heavy load, and that there were surely a hundred people in the vehicle.

"There are as many as you may see with your own eyes," Abba replied, wondering if there was a purpose in Jamal's inquiry; but probably it was truly only curiosity. "You are our good friend, you come and go at your pleasure, and you may see for yourself which among us are our old people, and which are new."

But Jamal did not keep him mystified long, for now he suggested that with so many new people, probably there would be more than were needed to work the lands of the settlement and more land could be utilized.

Then Abba knew it was indeed the question of the swamp again, to which Jamal and his numerous brothers and cousins made claim, though it had been untouched these many years except for a token patch of rice on the edge.

"There is plenty of land that is of no use to anyone," Abba said. "The swamp is only a place of pestilence and death. We will ask the government for it."

"Ah, but it is of use!" Jamal said. "For do we not earn our livelihood out of this swamp?"

"Indeed," said Abba. "This is something of which I did not know."

And Jamal replied, still smiling, "Indeed it is so. For in this swamp we cut these reeds for you." There was delight in his eyes, as when a man sets down the winning piece in a game of dominoes.

For several years Jamal had been hinting about the purchase of this land. When the colony had first been established, the Arab claim upon the swamp might have been bought for a few hundred pounds, but in those days the men in Jerusalem had insisted that there was no need to pay such baksheesh, since the government would surely turn the wasteland over to the Jews. Now the price of the dubious claim upon the worthless soil was already ten times what it had been. And even now, Abba knew, he would write again to Jerusalem that the land should be purchased, and drained, before the government gave it finally to the Arabs.

"You know it is against the new laws of the English for you to sell this land to us," Abba pointed out regretfully, as though he was hurt most of all by the loss of profit that this evil regulation would bring to his friend.

Ah, Jamal reminded him, the Jews were clever and could al-

63

ways arrange matters of law, for they were cleverer even than the English. For instance, if he and his kinsmen should merely say that they had never raised crops on this place, that might leave it free to the Jews. Or could they not say that they had already sold this place, even before the law came into being? For he and Abba had known each other and had spoken of this matter during many years, had they not? Surely the Jews could write such a thing on a paper, for the Jews knew how to do all manner of things with writing on paper. And to all this his cousins might now agree for a reasonable price.

They packed the gasoline tins on the donkey, one on each side, to balance, as Jamal had said. And their eyes met in shrewd understanding.

"Why do you need so much gasoline?" Abba asked. "To make your donkey go?"

Jamal smiled broadly. "We are buying a tractor like yours," he said.

Jamal mounted his donkey, and his boy Mustafa got up on the animal, too, and sat in front of his father. Daavid watched them as they rode away. On the path Jamal greeted Avram, who was bringing the new people to see the carpentry shop. Miriam was with them, and Weisbrod and Swobodniak followed, with Ziona and Dvora, and Blaustein, who was wearing shorts, which showed his thin crooked legs.

"*Shalom,* Daavid!" Avram said. "You got here ahead of us!" And he explained about the furniture-making factory, and said that the tables and chairs and lamps were sold all over Palestine. "On rainy days in winter we all work here," he said. "Perhaps some of you would like to learn this work."

Swobodniak asked whether it was profitable to have a factory on the farm, and Abba said, "From this shop we get one-fourth of our income." There were factories in many settlements, he said, and began to make a speech about the new machinery that had been ordered from America for enlarging the enterprise.

"If I want to work at a machine, I can work in the city for myself," Swobodniak said.

Yes, that was true, he could do so if he wished, Abba agreed.

Avram explained that the factory provided good light work for invalids, and for women, the whole year round.

64

"I'd rather work in the fields," Ziona declared.

Abba smacked his lips. "There is a girl!" He said he would show them where the big tractors were at work, and as they went to the fields Avram coaxed his father, "Tell them the tales of the real pioneers of thirty years ago, when crocodiles and man-eating jackals roamed these fields. Tell them how I was born in a tent, like an Arab."

Abba said, "If you listen to Avram, you must remember that as the *sabra* is taller than a Jew from Pinsk, so are his lies."

Daavid listened to their joking. It was the first time he had known a grown man together with his father. Often he had wondered if a father feels useless when his son grows up, if he then feels he is ready to die; but now he saw there was a good feeling between the older and the younger man.

The group came to an open field where a tractor was working. The driver was young Amos, who had been on the shore during the landing. His tractor was pulling an implement that had many small wheels in the earth, and Abba said these disks loosened the soil and made it ready for planting. He said everything came from America, the tractor, too. It was a very high tractor, with giant rubber wheels, like the wheels on an army truck for carrying tanks; and Amos sat above them all, as on a throne.

Swobodniak and Blaustein and Ziona were whispering together excitedly. Swobodniak was saying, "Of course it's not for us. It's for specialists."

And Blaustein said, "I was a mechanic, I can easily learn to drive a tractor."

"It's only for them," Swobodniak insisted. "We can work in the fields with our hands."

Then Ziona said, "Ask him!"

And Blaustein spoke up, "Can we become tractorists, too?"

"Why not?" Avram replied.

Ziona said excitedly, "And a girl? Can a girl become a tractorist, too?"

"Whatever a man can do, a woman can do," Avram said.

Abba looked at her fondly. "But there are things a woman can do that a man can't do," he declared, beaming. "That's what's important!" He patted Ziona. "Children, to build the homeland!" Abba was a man that liked all girls, Daavid decided. But why did

65

they all want to have children, even in the camps, even on the boat? Everybody was always talking about having more children. There were enough children in the world.

"Tractorists!" Abba said, still with his arm around Ziona. "That is the one thing in everybody's heart. We could build a homeland of tractorists alone!"

Now Amos was asking, "And you, Daavid, don't you want to stay here and become a tractorist?"

They wanted to keep him here. He saw himself sitting high up, like Amos, and driving the giant-wheeled machine over the long fields. And yet he put aside the wish; he would not let them keep him from what he had to do. "No," he replied, "I don't want to."

"But I do!" Ziona laughed, and Amos motioned to her. She clambered up on the machine and stood behind him holding on to his shoulders. He let her put one hand on a lever as they started off, and everyone joked at Ziona's joy.

The others all went on, walking with Abba. They came to the end of the fields, where the earth broke off and fell away sharply, forming a cliff over the river. Across the river was the Arab village, with houses made of earth. Far below, Daavid could see Jamal and Mustafa crossing the river, wading in deep as they walked beside their donkey.

It was the Jordan River, they said, and Dvora exclaimed over it, and wondered that a man could walk across it. Abba said that there were places where the river was deeper, but that there were also many such places where a man could walk across, "as in the time of Moses, and all our fathers, when they first came into Palestine."

"Was it here that they crossed?" Tirza asked.

"No," Dvora said, proud of her knowledge, "that was farther down, near Jericho."

The cliff over the river was covered with wild grass, and there were scattered red flowers growing among the grass. Then there was one fenced place with tall dark trees forming an enclosure, and Abba was taking everybody into that place. It was a cemetery.

Daavid stopped by the gate; he would not go in there. Miriam stood for a moment with him. "Aren't you coming inside,

Daavid?" she said. "There are the most beautiful trees here."

He told her, "I don't like the dead."

She left him and walked inside.

He found a stick and began to scratch things in the earth. He could hear Abba talking by the graves. He could just see him through the leaves of the intervening trees; Abba's large head with the white hair looked like a stone monument against the gray earth.

"The place where you want to be when you die," Abba said, "that is your true home. In the old times only old Jews came to Eretz Yisroel, because they wanted to die in this land. But in my time, we decided that young Jews could also come here, to live."

Abba said he had come to this very place a long time ago, as a young man, as young as they were; he had come from the city of Odessa, with other young people like himself, and they had made their way in horse-carts to the shores of Kinneret, because in those days there were no roads for trucks and busses and automobiles. They had sought this spot because "from the Torah, from our Bible, we knew there was once a garden of Eden by the waters of the Jordan. Figs and almonds and pomegranates and every kind of fruit, everything grew in this land. But after our forefathers were driven away, it was empty," Abba said. "For hundreds of years nobody tended this land." He told them to look in the distance, at Mount Hermon. It was the peak where the snow could still be seen, and Daavid also looked and saw the mountain, like a white-haired giant, another Abba, standing forever in the distance. "The waters from the Hermon came down, and made a swamp, and pests, and mosquitoes, and malaria, that's all that was here. The Arabs would not live here, they called it the bed of death, and even in Jamal's village on the hill, they were few, and always sick, a poor sick village."

The first year, Abba told them, everyone went down with malaria. "I went down, and got up. My wife went down, and she lies here. Too many died," he said. "We had to give up our settlement. We went away, and left this place."

And then he told how young pioneers had come again to this place. "Ten years ago they came here to try again. A new group of youth. With experts. With machinery. They didn't want to take me along. Too old. Ha! My son Avram was with them—a young pioneer already, and his father was too old! It's a good thing I came anyway. What did they know of malaria, and of swamps, and of Arabs? A son can still learn from his father!"

Daavid scratched lines in the earth with his stick. He did not even want to hear about young Avram and his father coming together to this place to build their home. Now he saw Avram, who had stopped somewhere behind; he was coming up the path, carrying a handful of the red flowers that he had picked.

Avram stopped and watched what Daavid was doing. "I didn't know you could write Hebrew," Avram said.

Daavid said, "I can't."

Avram dropped down, resting on one knee beside him, and traced over the lines Daavid had drawn with his stick. "But that's your name, Halevi," Avram said.

"My father showed me how to write it before he went away," Daavid told him.

"Did he show you how to write all the letters in the alphabet?" Avram asked.

"He was teaching me how to write," Daavid said. "My father can write everything."

"And do you remember some of the other letters, too?" Avram asked. "Can you read them?" He got up, and Daavid got up, too. As they talked, he went along with Avram. "I remember only a little," Daavid said.

Inside the enclosure, standing in front of a large gravestone with three names on it, Abba was telling how the three people had been killed in fighting here. Blaustein read the Hebrew names on the stones, "Reuven Hyman, Shlomo Barzelli, Sara Cohen," and Tirza said, "A girl, too. And her name was Cohen, like mine."

"What did they know of Arabs!" Abba said. There had been an attack in 1936.

"Arabs!" Blaustein repeated in his half-whisper, looking toward Jamal's village.

The attack had not come from there, Abba told them. But from Bedouin gangs that had been hired across the border, from Syria, where the Mufti's men were working openly with German agents. "They even attacked Jamal's village as well, for warning us."

Avram walked farther. Daavid followed him to an old grave-

68

stone, apart from the others, and Avram placed his flowers on the grave. "Can you read this name," he asked, "from what your father taught you?"

Daavid tried to make out the name. Perhaps it was another hero who had fought the raiders. The first letter was the same as in his own name—*ha.*

Miriam had come toward them and was watching him, too.

Avram helped him. "Hadassah," Avram read. "Hadassah Salmoni. She was my mother. She died here, a little after I was born."

Daavid felt bitter that Avram had purposely brought him here to show him this. He could have beat his fists on the stone and cried. He turned his face from them and went away quickly, anywhere, away.

Avram made a movement to go after the child.

"Leave him alone," Miriam said to Avram. "He has to learn that mothers die."

Alone, Daavid walked along the cliff where the earth dropped away to the river. There was a steep way down, and he followed it, half sliding. The bank was like a jungle, with reeds growing out of the muddy, stagnant pools. He looked above and could not see the people on the height; he was by himself. He did not know what made him want to be with people, and yet always want to break away from them. Now as he walked in this jungle Daavid again felt better to be alone, and yet he wondered whether Avram would come after him.

Then he heard some voices singing, and saw a group of men working in the thick growth, chopping away the vegetation, clearing the bank of the river. They were naked except for their shorts, and their backs were shining with sweat; some were standing in mud and ooze up to their knees. They were men from the settlement, but he saw Maccabee among them, working even harder today; and there was another one, who called, *"Shalom,* Daavid!" and grinned at him. Daavid saw that it was Lazar, without his beard!

Maccabee explained, like an expert, that these were the pestholes in which mosquitoes bred, and that malaria was carried by mosquitoes, and therefore the banks of the river had to be cleared, so the water could flow freely and wash away the stagnant breeding places of the insects. They would clear the riverbanks, as far as the Arab village, and beyond.

Then it was by the sickness from here, that Avram's mother had been killed.

And then Daavid saw Avram coming down to the place, but Avram had not come in search of him. The Palestinian stripped off his shirt, rolled up his trousers, and went to work with the others. "After this is all cleaned up," he explained to Daavid, "we'll spray everything with DDT. Just so you won't get malaria."

Daavid knew what DDT was. The Americans blew it under your clothes. And now Maccabee said the Americans also blew it from airplanes over entire fields, to kill everything that made sickness, in plants as well as in people. Perhaps, Maccabee said, they would become experts and even do this in Palestine—with airplanes. Perhaps some day Daavid would fly an airplane and spray the earth with DDT.

Or would he rather spray it with bombs? Lazar asked cheerfully.

Daavid did not want to be cheerful with them. He went farther along, toward the place where the Arabs crossed the river in coming from their village. The reeds grew very high here, but in one place an opening had been made, and he saw the Arab boy Mustafa cutting down the thick stalks and loading them on his donkey. Mustafa had a special curved knife for this work.

Daavid took his own knife out of his pocket. It was an army knife, given him by an American soldier. There were many things that folded into the knife: a screwdriver, a hole-puncher, a can-opener, and several blades. He began to cut a reed.

The Arab boy asked to see the knife. Daavid showed it to him.

Mustafa unfolded the hole-puncher and tried it on one of the stalks. It made a small clean hole in the reed. "This will make a nice flute," he said.

They sat down, and Mustafa showed Daavid how to make a flute.

When Shulamith woke that morning, she was filled with delight because of what she was going to do. She hurried to the schoolroom before anyone was there, and she wrote some numbers on her arm. This way she would be his sister. Then she ran out to find Daavid.

The little girl saw him, by the riverbank, with Mustafa. She ran toward him, laughing, and holding her hand over her numbers, so as to surprise him.

"Daavid, look!" She uncovered her secret. "Now I am your sister, and you are my brother, and my father and mother are your father and mother, because yours are dead!"

Daavid leaped up, wanting to destroy her. "They're not dead!" he screamed. "I don't want your father and mother! I don't want you! I have two sisters—my own!"

She began to cry and ran away.

Now Daavid felt as in the old times, in the woods. He could do whatever he wanted.

Beside him stood Mustafa and the donkey. "I have to go look for my family," Daavid said. "Do you want this knife for your donkey?"

The Arab boy fondled the knife, but hesitated, looking toward the village. He was worried that his father might not like the trade, Daavid saw.

"I thought she was your donkey," Daavid said.

Suddenly Mustafa smiled and pocketed the knife. "I will go with you," he said. "I know the best roads."

They mounted the donkey and started on their way.

Shulamith ran back to the yard, but she did not go to the children's house, for the other children might see what had happened. She ran to her parents' house; on the porch there was a basin of water, and she began to scrub the numbers from her arm.

Nahama came on her there. The child was tearful, and the numbers still showed on the red scrubbed part of her arm.

"Daavid didn't want me," she sobbed. "I wanted to be Daavid's sister, and he drove me away!"

There was little that Nahama could do to ease the wound. "Naturally, Daavid wants his own sister," she said. "He wants you to be his friend and his comrade."

She helped Shulamith wash off the numbers.

Later in the morning Nahama found a moment to speak to Miriam. The young woman had already asked to have her name put on the worksheet, and she was assigned to the dairy. Nahama found her carrying fodder in the cattleyard. Miriam came to the fence, wiping her forehead on her sleeve. She looked less strained, though the flies were buzzing around her hair, and her bare legs were bitten. "You'd better wear a scarf on your head if you're going to work with the cattle," Nahama advised. "And stop in the clothes-room and ask Sara for a pair of long trousers."

"Yes, I know," Miriam said.

Nahama told what had happened with Shulamith and Daavid, trying to relate it more as an incident among children, tender and touching as it might have been, than as something serious. But, nevertheless, she suggested that they ought to try to find a way to bring Daavid together with the children of the settlement. Perhaps Miriam could help him to understand that all the children here really felt themselves like brothers and sisters. She herself would try with Shulamith and the other children. "I am sure she still wants to make friends with him," Nahama said. "A pity that it should have started so badly."

But there was no use in minimizing the incident to Miriam. She knew the boy too well, Nahama saw. The young woman felt his behavior from within herself.

"Even if Shulamith does try again, it won't help. Daavid won't let the children make friends with him," Miriam said. "He won't be able to adjust himself here. How can he? He must resent them all, he must hate them, because they have their parents."

"But he has you," Nahama said.

The young woman looked at her directly, with that unblinking clarity that was so frightening because it was so unanswerable. "He must resent me," Miriam said, "because I am not his mother."

Tentatively Nahama brought forward a thought that had been in her mind. "In other settlements, in Shomer Ha-Emek, for example," she said, "it worked out quite naturally. The refugee children attached themselves to families. They simply did it of their own accord, little by little, and now it is hard to tell the difference between the natural children of a family and the additions. Of course, there were a few difficult cases." But Miriam, she saw, was following her own inner line of thought, as though she already knew that this method would not work with Daavid.

"He should be among children who have no more than he has," Miriam said. "He has to learn to live through other orphans, children like himself. If there was a place, with other refugee orphans—"

For a moment the argument seemed logical to Nahama. "There is such a place, the children's village, near Haifa," she found herself saying. But then she caught herself up. "But you wouldn't want him to go there." She looked steadily at Miriam. It was already too late, she saw, the idea was already forming in Miriam. Nahama threw in the first argument that came to her mind. "What would you do without him?"

She had said the wrong thing again. There was something in Miriam, and in all of them, that made one say the wrong thing. You could speak to them, and have contact, and suddenly the contact would be gone and you continued speaking but as though with different meanings for the same words. Perhaps it was because they had not been permitted to have their own feelings for so long a time.

The flies were all around the girl's hair. "Here, borrow my kerchief," Nahama said, unbinding it and giving it to Miriam. She was afraid for an instant that the girl would refuse even this.

But Miriam took it and thanked her, smiling absently.

After work Miriam looked for Daavid in the children's house. He was not there, nor in the dining-hall, nor by the pool where the children swam. She looked for him in the barnyard and among the sheds. At last she became alarmed. She asked a passing comrade where she might find Avram.

He had moved out of his room and was living in one of the tents under the trees by the gate. Avram had not seen the boy since morning, but surely, he said, Daavid must have been seen. He would ask in the shower-room, where he was just going.

Maccabee was in the showers. He had last seen Daavid with the Arabs who were cutting papyrus reeds by the river, he said. And Avram felt the alarm spreading automatically among the newcomers. Swobodniak's eyes had already taken on their feverish, knowing glint. "Of course. The Arabs—"

And Maccabee began, "If they've—"

73

"Don't be foolish," Avram said. "Perhaps he went home with them. Anyway, I'll ride over there."

It was a pity that they came with the myth already grown in them.

He saddled the black horse Gedalia, which he had bought from Jamal's cousin Nassim, remembering how one time a Bedouin had stolen the animal, and how another of the cousins had seen the horse, far beyond Nazareth, and had come and shown him where to recover the horse. Naturally, for a suitable gift.

And as he rode Avram thought of ways in which he could bring the newcomers to understand the complex way of life with the Arabs, and how one must be at once always friendly and always on guard. It might be a good idea to teach them a little Arabic, perhaps once a week, even as they began to learn Hebrew. But Zev would surely argue that this would confuse them, and it would be better to wait. Perhaps it would be best to select one among them for training in Arabic and in the ways of the Arab people, someone he could take with him to their village occasionally.

Avram had just got down to the river when he saw Jamal splashing across on his white mare. *"Marḥaba, Jamal,"* Avram greeted him. "I was just coming to you. Have you seen anything of our new little boy? Daavid, he is called."

"Marḥabtein," Jamal replied. "And I am coming to you. Mustafa has not come home, and the donkey is with him."

It was clear, then, what had happened. The boys could not have gone too far; yet in a day they could go far enough. As for the way they had gone, Jamal said that would not be difficult to discover, for many would have seen them passing, and the way Mustafa knew best was the road to Nazareth.

First the boys rode along the edge of the lake. The donkey trotted nimbly, and as they rode Daavid began to feel a singing inside of him. It came from all that was around him. There was a singing from the lake itself, with the fishing boats not far from the shore, and the blueness that looked so warm. And the movement of the atmosphere itself felt good, for it was no longer warm air that pressed upon him and pressed him down, but air that was like clean clothes.

74

A truck filled with children from another settlement passed them, and the children were all singing the song of the lake that Yehudith and all the others had sung on the truck as they had come to Makor Gallil. Two Arabs with many camels passed them, and the camel bells were ringing. Above the hills there were thin little furrows of clouds, like fluted paper.

It was a place, Daavid felt, like no place else he had been. It was good that his father had chosen this land and this place; and his father could not be very far from here. He was surely going to him now.

Mustafa took out his flute and began a tune that was like the donkey walking and camels walking. Daavid also took his flute, and one by one the notes came, and the tune itself. The music went as the donkey walked, and they passed a place where the fishermen were mending their wide nets, some of which were spread by the water, and others hung from low branches of trees. They were not dressed as Arabs, but were bare, and brown, wearing only shorts, and Mustafa said, *"Yehudim."* They were Jews, and called *shalom* to the boys, and Daavid answered, *"Shalom."*

The boys traveled on. But after a time the donkey would not walk to the music, but went more slowly, and at last came to a stop. Mustafa beat her neck with a stick, but still the donkey would not move.

"Why won't she go?" Daavid said.

Mustafa slid from the animal's back and walked around, looking at her, just as a driver looks at a truck that has stopped.

"I think maybe she is a little bit sick," Mustafa said. "She does not want to carry us any more."

Daavid also climbed down from the animal and studied her. Mustafa did not seem worried. "We will walk for a while," he said. "Then she will be better."

They walked, and the donkey walked with them. They were passed by a convoy of great military trucks, each with a soldier at a machine gun mounted over the driver's cab, and some of the trucks were filled with soldiers.

All big highways were mainly for armored cars and military trucks; this had always been so, on the roads of Europe, too; this was why the broad fine roads had been built, he knew. Before the liberation in Europe, when military vehicles appeared on the road, it had been the time to hide; but after the liberation military vehicles were good, and sometimes they even gave rides; he had even ridden in them himself, with Maccabee. But here in Palestine Daavid was not sure how to feel; from the way the truck had brought them without lights at night, he thought, things were more like before the liberation, and therefore it was best to keep out of sight and out of the way of military vehicles.

He was glad when Mustafa said he knew a short cut, and they left the road and began to climb the hills. Daavid believed these were the same hills that Avram had shown him on the map, where the Maccabees had fought. He could see caves far up in the sheer side of the mountains, and he wished for someone who could tell him about these caves. But now the donkey was reluctant even to walk, and Daavid had to push him from behind.

They passed close to an encampment of black tents, where many Arab children were playing, and women were walking with large jugs of water balanced on their heads. Even if his father were like an Arab, living in such a tent, he would go out and tend the sheep; he would be content.

Farther up the donkey stopped altogether and would not be pushed. Then she lay down.

Still, Mustafa did not seem to be worried. He took a flat piece of bread from the sack that hung over the donkey's back; broke it, and gave Daavid half. The bread was dry, and round, and tasted like the matzoth that they had eaten on the boat.

"We must wait until she is ready to go again," Mustafa said.

When Jamal and Avram came upon the boys the donkey had already given birth to her foal. Still filled with surprise, Daavid carried the little animal out toward them. The foal was black, not gray like his mother; his hair was damp.

"I didn't know she was a mother," Daavid said.

At such a moment the men could not be angry. But the journey was ended.

Mustafa took the army knife from his pocket and held it out to Daavid. "It is yours," he said. "I did not take you as far as the city of your father. We are not going."

But Daavid would not accept the knife. "You tried to go," he said.

76

The men saw, then, how the boys had made their bargain. Jamal was frowning, for he was not pleased with his son. He considered the foal, which was to have been for Mustafa. "Then let this little one belong to Daavid," Jamal said.

The legs of the little animal were like rods of electricity, thrusting already with surprising energy against Daavid's hands. He saw that Mustafa's father was angry with his son, but there was no anger from Avram. And it was natural that Avram did not have the same anger. For Daavid was not a son who had gone away from him. And therefore Daavid felt he had not done wrong, but only what he needed to do. He did not need to be punished, like Mustafa, for running away from home. He would accept the exchange of the little animal for his knife, and for the failure of the journey.

"We can feed him with milk from a bottle," Avram said. "Come, we'll take him home."

Avram lifted Daavid up on the black horse and gave him the little animal to hold in front of him. Then Avram mounted behind, and they were like one rider.

Daavid saw Mustafa lead out the gray mother donkey, while Jamal mounted on his horse. Mustafa was still holding the army knife in his hand, and as they parted, Mustafa smiled again to show that, nonetheless, he did not feel he had made a bad trade.

Daavid wondered whether Avram would show anger once they were away from the others, but Avram seemed to let it pass, as if Daavid had only gone out a little way with Mustafa and the donkey and would have come home except for the trouble of the donkey giving birth.

He felt Avram close behind him as they rode, large over him. And the little animal just come into life stirred and nuzzled its head against Daavid, seeking warmth.

Avram said, "He will grow up quickly. Then you'll have your own donkey. Then you can go all over Palestine to look for your family if you want."

It was good that he had his back to Avram, for Daavid did not want the man to see how he felt. In this moment he felt that he could almost wait the long time that Avram had asked of him, because this was the first time that someone had agreed in his search. With Miriam, Daavid was never sure. Sometimes he even felt that she did not believe his people were here, or anywhere.

It was coming toward sunset now, and the sun was on the hills on the other side of Kinneret; they were red, as though painted on paper, and the sea was as it appeared in a good dream, floating with your father and mother in a sailboat.

They passed below the caves, and he asked Avram whether these were the caves of the Maccabees. No, Avram said, but these caves had been used by the Sicarii, who carried daggers under their cloaks and fought like partisans.

"Against the Greeks?" Daavid asked. "Like the Maccabees?"

"No," Avram explained. "In the time of the Sicarii the Greeks had already been driven out, but there were Romans. The Sicarii came out at night and raided the camps of the Roman soldiers."

"Like the Irgun," Daavid said.

"Where did you learn about the Irgun?" asked Avram.

"Amos and Maccabee were talking," Daavid said, and he glanced back at Avram to see if it was in any way wrong. But Avram was only smiling his small faraway smile.

"How could anyone get up to those caves?" Daavid asked.

There were narrow ledges and ways of climbing, Avram told him.

"Did you ever go up there and see them?"

Yes, Avram said, when he was a boy he had climbed all over these mountains and looked into many of the caves. There were even some caves that could be reached only by means of a rope. Among them, he said, were caves of Christian saints, who had lived their lives there, high in the wall of the hill. There were also caves in other parts of Eretz Yisroel, he said, and the most wonderful place was the high stronghold of Masada, in the southern wilderness, where the Judeans under Bar Kochba held out to the last man.

"Against the Greeks or the Romans?" Daavid asked.

"The Romans," Avram said.

"Did you go to Masada?" Daavid asked.

Yes, Avram said, he had gone there on a hike with a group of boys from his *kibbutz*. Sometime Daavid would surely do the same thing, perhaps with his friend Maccabee. And then Daavid would see Masada and other places, too.

It was agreeable having Avram riding so close behind him, like

78

a voice that could answer all things, and it was easier, too, that he did not have to see Avram's face, and that Avram did not see his face, for Daavid felt things moving tumultuously inside of him, and did not yet know about all these new things. They had something to do with the warriors, whom he could see, great uncles of the past, dark and tall and strong-boned men, like Avram and Zev, climbing about on these hills, carrying their spears.

"Was King Daavid here, too?" he asked.

Yes, Avram said, Daavid had been this far, too, when he was king. It was he who had made all this land a part of Israel, after defeating the Assyrians, but mostly he had stayed in Jerusalem.

They turned on a downcurve in the road, and Daavid could see Makor Gallil far below.

"And who lives in the caves now?" Daavid asked. "Does anyone live in them?"

"No," Avram said. "I don't think so. But they can always be used."

Something in Avram's voice made Daavid turn to look at his face. Avram was smiling again, way behind his eyes, as if some thought had pleased him. "They are still good places," he said.

"Even against tanks," Daavid said, and this time they smiled together. It made the same warm feeling in Daavid as when the little foal thrust out its legs. There had been, as Avram said, Assyrians and Greeks and Romans, and now there were British.

He saw a battle, and partisans holding out to the last man against the tanks and the flame-throwers, and his father was there, with Avram and Zev and their whole troop, and he was the ammunition carrier, running to them from the stores in the back of the cave.

They left the road for a short cut across the stony, vacant fields. The whole long valley seemed vast and desolate as the descending light lay upon it. There were only the little dark areas of the few settlements, where their groves made a pattern of shadow. All else was empty. It was as though in all those wars everyone had been killed, and no one had come back.

"Nobody lives here," Daavid said to Avram. "Why is everything so dead? Did people live here once?"

Avram laughed softly. "Yes, many people," he said. And as Avram leaned a little bit forward, moving his hands to shake the reins, Daavid felt the warm enveloping pressure of the man's arms around his body.

Near the gate Miriam was waiting, and in a moment all the children came running, excitedly gathering around Daavid, exclaiming over the newborn foal.

"Look what Daavid has brought!" they cried. "Daavid brought him! Daavid, Daavid, where did you find him!"

They were all around him, like friends. They thought of a thousand things, how to feed the animal, where he should sleep, what to do with him when he was grown. Gideon even said he would get his father to build a little cart.

Shulamith ran to get some milk, and Maccabee came and said he would help make a bed in the stable.

But before Daavid went with them, they had to know, and especially Miriam had to know, that what he had started to do, he would do. "When he is grown," Daavid said, "Avram promised I could ride him all over Palestine and find my father's house."

Then he went with the children who clustered around him as he carried the little foal.

At once Miriam turned upon Avram. "Did you tell him he could do that?" she demanded.

"It will keep him home for a while—until the little donkey grows up," Avram said. "And by then—"

It was an optimist, then, with whom she had to deal. "Why must you do this to him!" Miriam demanded. "Can't you see that instead of helping him to get rid of his obsession, you're only making it all the stronger! His family is surely dead. The only way to help him is to make him realize the truth."

"After all," Avram said, "some people have found their families. A few people did survive—even as you did, and Daavid."

"Not even one in a thousand," she said. And at the same moment she was angry with herself for having answered him in his own terms, for any such speculation was an evasion of the real problem of the boy's obsession.

"Still, there is a chance," he persisted.

She wanted to walk away from this sickness of hope, which brought a kind of revulsion in her. It was the same sick hope that

80

was in the people even when they were already in the dim cattle trains, eying each other, measuring each other, measuring the muscles, the thickness and weight of flesh. For if ten of those in the cargo were to survive, which ten would it be? Which had the thickest flesh to melt, the largest store of water in the flesh to endure thirst? And when the line-up of the survivors came before the appraising eyes, who would have the firmest muscles, the straightest bones, to survive that competition? Who would succeed, survive, be among the five per cent selected for slavery rather than to walk the furnace?

But how could he know, how could anyone here know, what was real?

She tried to say it within his own dimension, as in simplifying some truth of nature. "Daavid doesn't even remember his father's name," she said to Avram. "He could never recognize them, or they him. How would he ever find them, even if one of them were alive?"

But for this also he had an answer. There was a special search bureau in Jerusalem, he said, collecting lists of all the survivors in all the camps and towns. "I've already thought of writing to them about Daavid."

Let him do it, then, and put an end to this distraction, at least for himself! Perhaps afterward she would be able to get through him, perhaps then some way could be found truly to help the child in his problem. "At least," she said, "don't tell Daavid about this— this search. It's cruel and dangerous to cling to these last hopes of miracles."

"We are crazy people here, Miriam," he said. "We believe that for some people, especially for children, it is better to hope, and be wrong, than to have no hope at all."

In the stable Maccabee arranged a warm berth of straw. And then Shulamith came running with a nipple-bottle filled with milk. "It's even sterilized," she said, "from the baby's house. Rivka gave it to me." She put the bottle to the foal's lips. It pulled its head away.

"Eat! Eat!" the children called to the little animal.

Shulamith tried again, but still the baby donkey refused. It stood with its legs far apart, and the front legs trembled a little. Everybody wanted to try feeding it with the bottle; they all put their hands on the foal, petting and coaxing him.

"I'll feed him myself!" Daavid cried and seized the bottle. He pushed it against the donkey's muzzle, following the little beast's head as it turned from side to side. The donkey backed away, and Daavid pushed the bottle after it.

"I know what to name him," Gideon declared. "Balaam."

"What's that?" Daavid demanded.

"A donkey in the Bible," Gideon said. "He talked."

"That was the name of the man," Shulamith said, "not the donkey."

"Here Balaam, Balaam!" the children cried. "Eat, Balaam! Eat, Balaam!"

Then Daavid thought of a way to make the animal eat. He squeezed milk on his finger and rubbed it against the foal's lips. Still it would not touch the bottle.

"Stupid animal," Maccabee said. "Doesn't even know enough to eat. Well, I do," he joked, getting up to go to the dining-hall. He called Daavid to come with him.

Daavid tried again, forcing the nipple into the donkey's mouth.

Slowly the animal's legs collapsed, and it lay on the straw. A strange small sound, not even like that of a donkey, came from him.

"Balaam! Balaam!" they called, all gathering still closer, and stroking and stroking the donkey.

"I think he is going to die," Gideon declared.

"He wants his mother," Shulamith said. "That's why he's crying. Balaam won't eat unless it's from his mother."

Then bitterness overcame Daavid. He jumped up, shouting at them all. "Go away! He's mine! I'll give him his name! I'll feed him! I'll take care of him!"

The children rose and looked at him without saying anything. Then they all went away.

When he was alone, he knelt down on the straw and tried once more to feed the baby donkey. But it would not touch the milk bottle. He told himself it was not hungry. At last he got up and left it and went out of the stable.

But he heard it crying, and he could not go away. Daavid went back and picked it up in his arms. He started across the fields toward the river.

It was already dusk, and as he walked the foal grew heavy in his arms. Once he set it down to see if it would come after him, but it only stood, helpless, its legs apart, and trembling, so he picked it up again and took the long way down to the riverbank. He found the place where the Arabs crossed and went into the water. The current was strong, and the stones were slippery; he could feel them through his sandals. The foal was frightened and struggled in his arms. The water came to his knees, and then almost to his waist, and he held the foal as high as he could, but still its feet were wet in the river.

At last he came to the other side and started up to the Arab village. The lanes were narrow, and on both sides were high walls made out of gray earth, with doorways in them. He had never been in such a place. From these lanes and from behind the walls enemies might come. Abba and Avram had said that this village was friendly, and Jamal and Mustafa were friendly. Still, Daavid remembered all that had been said about Arabs in the camps in Italy, in the months of waiting to come to Palestine.

It was nearly dark now, and the lanes were empty. In one doorway a bearded Arab looked at him silently, and his eyes were not friendly. But Daavid walked directly ahead and passed the man. Then there were some very old Arabs sitting against a wall. "Jamal?" he asked, and one of them pointed to a doorway.

Abba was sitting with Jamal on a mat in his courtyard. They were smoking water pipes and playing dominoes. At intervals between moves they spoke of the matter of the little swamp, where the river divided. Jamal had been talking to his cousins, he told Abba, and some of them were now afraid, especially Tallil was afraid, to sell his claim to the Jews. It was mostly because of the stories about the sheik in Tulkarem who had been assassinated a few days ago. They said they did not want to be found with their faces stuffed with earth and bullet holes in the backs of their heads.

"It is also said that an angry husband shot him," Abba suggested, for the habits of the assassinated sheik had been well known all over Palestine.

Jamal granted that this was a possibility. Still, the sheik had

83

owned a great deal of land, by the sea, on the sands, and this land was now in the hands of Jews.

"But it was land that he got from the government for nothing," Abba reminded Jamal. "It was only sand. And from the sale he became rich, and bought three automobiles, and married the daughters of effendis."

Jamal laughed, and said much good the wives had done the man if he still lusted after the wives of others, as one would have to believe if it were true that he had been killed because of a woman instead of by followers of the Mufti over the sale of land.

"And even if a man were killed by the Mufti's followers in Tulkarem," Abba pointed out, "why should another be afraid, in Abiyah? The Mufti's family is thick in Tulkarem, but fortunately there are few Husseinis in this region."

At this Jamal grew serious. Things would be difficult in Abiyah now, he said, for a teacher had been sent to establish a school for the children.

"But there is no evil in a school," Abba said. "Who is the teacher?"

"He is a Khaldi, from Jerusalem. And they are tied by many marriages to the Mufti's family, the Husseinis." One had to wait and see about this teacher, he said. It would be difficult to speak further regarding the sale of land in the village.

"The Husseinis themselves have sold land, as you know," Abba said. "And they are not tillers, but sit in the cities, in Egypt and Syria. Then why should they not allow you to sell?"

Jamal shook his head over his friend's lack of wisdom. "When they do not allow any land to be sold," he pointed out, "you will pay more. And when you pay much more, they also will sell."

"Then why do you listen to them?"

"I will tell you what my cousin said," Jamal offered. "He said, 'It is not my land that I will sell, but my life, after what was done in Tulkarem.' But," Jamal added, "this cousin is a friend, and he would sell if he could receive enough money to buy a house and live forever in America."

Abba sighed. It would be a long, long affair. Then he saw Daavid come into the compound, carrying the foal.

The mother donkey was tied to a little pepper tree that grew in the yard. She brayed, and Daavid felt the foal trying to jump from

84

his arms. He gave the baby back to its mother. The foal began at once to suckle.

"Balaam wouldn't eat. He wanted his mother," Daavid said to Mustafa.

Jamal and Abba had come forward. "When he is big," Jamal said, "he will leave his mother. And then he will be yours."

Abba put his arm around Daavid, and they said their farewells and started for home.

During the night Daavid felt like a sick dog who is all alone. He thought of the foal, and even the little beast was not alone. He could not stay in the room where the parents of Gideon and Menahem had been sitting on the beds of the boys, until their children slept. He crept out and walked until he was at the edge of the cliff, over the river. He sat there for a long time.

When Miriam found him, she said only, "Come back to bed now, Daavid. There are mosquitoes at night. You might get malaria."

"I don't care," he said. He didn't care what happened to him, but he let her take him back.

Avram had a turn on the watchtower that night. Though it was not very late, the yard was deserted, as everyone was in the dining-hall at a meeting of welcome for the newcomers. Then he saw the shadowy forms of Miriam and the boy as they came from the fields. He climbed down, and finding Moshe reading in the lower room, asked him to take the watch for a while.

Avram saw the young woman take Daavid into the children's house. He waited until she came out, after putting the child to bed. Miriam did not seem surprised to meet him. "I must talk to you," she said. "Something must be done for Daavid."

From within the children's house they could hear a small sound. It was not sobbing, but a faint, muffled sound, which was worse.

"He can't remain here," Miriam said. "In a single day he has quarreled with all the children and has tried to run away. Now everything here will seem even more hateful to him because he has failed." She said that she had heard from Nahama of a children's village, and she had made up her mind that it was the place for Daavid.

"You think we should send him away?" Avram repeated. "Is that what you want?"

"What I want is not the question," she said. "He needs to be with other boys who are like himself."

Surely, Avram argued, it would not be good for the boy to leave his only friends, to be defeated so soon in his new life.

But she had considered everything. The boy would have only a greater sense of defeat if the thing had to be done later. And he already felt deserted here, as his friends from Europe became absorbed in their new lives.

"In any case," Avram said, "it is not a matter that we alone can decide. We must discuss it with the others."

"Why?" she demanded. "They don't know Daavid. How can they decide what he needs?"

"Because here," he said, "we are all responsible for each other. It will have to come before a meeting."

"It can't wait," Miriam said. "You see yourself that he has reached a crisis."

Avram wondered if the crisis was not also in Miriam, if in deciding for this separation she did not need to have it done quickly while her resolution was still strong. It might be best for her to have the question over with at once. He did not think she would have her way. "Everyone is in the dining-hall, welcoming your group," he said. "You can bring it before them now."

They walked together to the meeting.

The Sabbath tablecloths were spread, and fruit and sweets had been set out. Many of the newcomers were still admiring the identity cards that had just been given to them, marveling at the speed with which the photographs, taken in the morning, had been completed. They were comparing their cards with those of the comrades of Makor Gallil, declaring that the true could not be told from the false.

"Now we are really Palestinians!" Maccabee enthusiastically announced, stopping Avram just inside the door and displaying his card. "Look! His Majesty's Government protects us!"

Chayim, the truck driver, was in the midst of a speech that was intended to be satirical, consoling the newcomers in their longing for the life they had left in Europe, and assuring them that things

86

were not too different in Palestine after all; they would find much to remind them of the cherished camps that had for so long been their homes. "Even here with us, you will live behind barbed wire, comrades. The only difference is that instead of being put there by our enemies to keep us in, we put it there ourselves, to keep our enemies out." But in case they should become homesick for a real concentration camp, he told them that they need not despair, for periodically the British would come to search the colony and cart off the lucky ones, picked because they smelled suspicious, to a British concentration camp, at a place called Latrun, built especially for their benefit as an exact replica of German camps. It was complete with towers and searchlights, and he was reliably informed that German experts would soon be imported to build a crematorium. At Latrun, he assured them, they would feel entirely at home. And then there was a special life attainable only to the selected few: for just as the Germans had made selections in the main camps, of groups to be sent out to special secret camps in unknown places, so the British would occasionally make a selection at Latrun, and the lucky candidates would be shipped off to the desert of Eritrea, and never be heard from again.

They were pleased at his humor. The young people laughed at each point, and Chayim happily continued.

Avram took Miriam up to the front, where Zev and Abba and several other members of the central committee sat at the first table, facing the room. Avram managed to get the attention of Zipporah, who was acting as secretary; she leaned over to them. "Miriam has an important question to bring before the comrades," he said.

"But this is a special occasion, a celebration," she said. "Can't it wait for a meeting?"

"She says it is urgent." And he explained that the matter concerned Daavid.

With her habit of explaining what the listener already knew, Zipporah said that such a question had to come first of all before the children's committee; the committee then could decide the matter themselves, or bring it before the central committee of the settlement, which again could dispose of the problem, or, if necessary, bring it before a general meeting.

"Of course, of course," Avram agreed. "But our new comrades

don't understand our procedure yet, and to them everything seems urgent."

No, Zipporah believed that the refugees should not be pampered, should learn discipline from the first.

Chayim had finished. Miriam, seeing what was happening, did not wait. She arose just as Abba, who was presiding with overflowing good will, was about to introduce another welcomer.

Abba leaned toward her, and recognized her, but first made a little speech. He was happy not only because he saw before him so many healthy young faces, where years ago there had been only a few lonely desolate sick souls; he was happy not only because the remnants had been brought out of Europe, but because Makor Gallil was being enriched, enhanced, yes, Makor Gallil was not only the benefactor but the beneficiary, receiving such eager young hands, such beautiful young girls! And now he was glad that one of them wanted to speak.

"I have a matter to bring before the membership," Miriam declared, and briefly stated Daavid's case. She tried to make it seem a report and a conclusion rather than a question to be discussed.

"It is better that he be sent immediately to live with other boys like himself." Surely they could see that every day he would build up a stronger resentment toward the other children. Only among orphans could he learn to live as an equal. When he was adjusted, when he knew how to live, he could come back to Makor Gallil.

But it was as she had feared. An interminable analysis began, not only from those who had come with Daavid, but also from the settlers of Makor Gallil, as if he were already part of their commune.

Some tended to minimize the whole thing—naturally the boy had had a little difficulty on his first day, but he would get used to the place. Others embarked on philosophic discussions of the relation of the parent to the child in the commune; perhaps this whole incident with Daavid showed that there was already too strong an emphasis on family life within the commune, and that the basic feeling of comradeship, of brotherhood and sisterhood, among all the children was lacking. This led to a side debate on the whole question of the family, with Sara, Chayim's wife, taking the opposite view, declaring that, if anything, family life had to be emphasized further, and that probably this was exactly what seemed lacking to Daavid, that he had seen their commune as a place where children lived too much separately, and that was why he wanted to run away to find a real family life.

Hillel rose to attack this as an emotional view. He began an abstruse dissertation, linking their treatment of children to their socialist goals, and then launched into a controversial discussion of child care in the Soviet Union, only to be howled down by one of the girls who accused him of being a bachelor.

Zipporah declared that in any case the whole question should not be decided by the *kibbutz* but by the intersettlement educational committee, whose next meeting would be two weeks hence.

More than an hour had passed. Some of the comrades were half asleep, their heads on their arms. Several of the women knitted busily. In a far corner Amos was helping Ziona spell out the headlines of the Hebrew daily, *Davar*.

And the child was probably lying awake, staring at the darkness. Miriam arose, impatiently. "The problem must be settled now," she insisted.

"All boys run away sometimes," Abba temporized. "It's natural. Even in the homeland."

And Zev now spoke. These problems could not be settled by meetings, he said. He recalled how it had been with the Teheran children—the orphans who had arrived in Palestine during the war, after a year of wandering through Asia and Arabia. "When we heard they were coming, I was living in Shomer Ha-Emek. We held meeting after meeting, sitting up half the night, debating whether we should keep them as a separate group or mix them in among our own children; should we do this or that, and the problems of adjustment seemed insoluble. Well, they came, we received thirty of them, and inside of two weeks they had solved all the problems themselves, quite naturally. They made friends, they adopted themselves into families, and in a few months you couldn't tell one of them from one of our own children. So it will be with Daavid."

Amos agreed. "Keep him here, give him time to get used to us."

A murmuring and buzzing spread all around, and they relaxed, as though the matter were disposed of.

Miriam could endure it no longer. "You've been arguing for an hour and a half, each according to how he thinks things ought to be," she accused them. "The matter as it stands is that the boy cannot remain here. He has already made enemies of the children, and he is in a desperate mood. I found him alone by the swamp. You are not thinking of him, but of yourselves. It's not for his sake that you want to keep him, but for yourselves, to feel that you are helping him."

"For ourselves?" Maccabee picked up her words, shouting. "Who has he, what has he, except us! We all have nothing but each other, and Daavid is one of us! We slept in the snow together, going over the Alps. He is a comrade, a little brother. Why on earth should he go to live somewhere else? He belongs with us, he is the same as we are!"

This was the hardest to answer. She felt Avram looking at her. She would not let anyone see that young Maccabee's words resounded within herself—a comrade, a little brother, a child.

He was the same, yes! she declared, for everyone who had come out alive bore the same sickness. But in some it was worse, and in the child Daavid it was worse than in any of them. "That is why he can't stay here with us. He is a child, and we are stronger. We can manage, and he cannot. He needs special help." Stonily she faced Abba. "You said yesterday we could leave if we wanted to. I will take the boy to the children's colony tomorrow."

For an instant no one spoke. Then Nahama helped her. "I believe it is as serious as Miriam says." Nahama proposed that the boy be sent to the children's village for a trial period. They gave in, most of them raising their hands slowly, reluctantly.

Chapter Five

When Daavid was told, he was not unhappy. For he was going, and to be going was the beginning of his search.

The truck was taking furniture to Haifa in the morning, and

90

Avram also had to go there, to buy DDT. Miriam was sent to accompany Daavid.

It was just after breakfast, and the comrades had not yet returned to their tasks. They crowded around, wishing him well. "You'll come back to us!" Dvora cried out to him, and Maccabee declared, "When we build our own settlement, you'll come with us, Daavid!"

Little Shulamith ran after the truck and waved, and her mother was carrying the baby in her arms, and the baby waved too, laughing happily.

This time it was day when the truck passed through the land. They all sat together on the broad driver's seat. Chayim said he would risk it as far as Haifa. They went on a new road, driving for a long time alongside the lake, farther than he had gone with Mustafa. And then they came to a town, which Avram said was Tiberias. He said it had been a Roman town, but before that it had had other names, and had been the place where the Torah was written when the rabbis were driven from Jerusalem. There were the ruins of thick walls of black stone, with round towers and fortifications.

But it was a small town, with only one street. There were both Arabs and Jews in this town, Avram said. Daavid did not feel that his family could be living here, though sometime he might return to search if he would not find them anywhere else. Then the truck went up the hill.

It went over hills where hardly anybody lived. Avram said that once there had been trees on all these hills, and many villages, but the Turks had cut down the trees, and then the rains had washed away the soil, because there were no longer any tree roots to hold the rainwater and keep the ground firm.

Daavid added to what he had known before, Greeks and Assyrians and Romans, and now there were Turks, too, and all of them had been enemies in this land.

Then the truck came down toward a vast warm valley, and all the fields were cultivated and looked like oblong strips of colored paper, green and red, yellow and black, and there were clusters of small white houses. This was a Jewish valley, Avram said. This was the Emek, and when Daavid saw this part of the land, he felt

91

sure. Yes, they were here, they were alive, he could feel them living somewhere in this land. As the truck passed through the Jewish villages Avram read the names of the places and told him their meanings, and Daavid tried to remember all this.

There was a village called Gideon, the same name as the boy in his room at the settlement. "Is he named for this place?" Daavid asked. No, Avram told him, the place and the boy were both named after the same person, a captain in ancient Israel, Gideon, who had driven the Midianites out of the land.

"The Midianites were people who came and stole our crops," Avram explained. After years of raiding, they had come in great numbers, with an entire army, to take not only the crops but the land itself. "They were here in this valley, all camped in these fields, thousands of them, with their swords and their spears, and with their supplies of war on their camel trains, all ready for battle."

All the farmers had taken to the hills, Avram said, but at Gideon's call they came to drive out the invader. And Gideon was only a farmer himself, but he wanted to save his land, and without shedding the blood of his comrades. So he selected the bravest of his people, to go with him on a night raid, rather than risk all of his people in an open war on the plain, against the superior numbers and superior arms of the Midianites.

The truck had passed the village now, and was on a long straight road that lay across the open farmland.

"Gideon took three hundred men with him that night," Avram continued. "They came down from those hills, facing us, and each man carried a trumpet, and in his other hand he carried a jar in which a lamp was hidden. They divided into three companies and surrounded the camp of the Midianites. Then, at a signal from Gideon, each man put his trumpet to his lips and blew. And at the same time they smashed the jars in which their lamps were hidden and brought out the burning lamps."

Daavid knew it was like suddenly using flashlights to blind and frighten the enemy.

"The Midianites were taken by surprise," Avram said, "and they were frightened and confused, and they seized their swords and began to fight wildly in the dark, and they fought against their own men."

92

"Just like the British shoot at each other in Jerusalem," Chayim said, "when they hear a noise at night and think it's the Irgun."

"And so it was," Avram said, "that Gideon's three hundred men drove out all the thousands of Midianites."

They came to another settlement, and there Chayim said he had to deliver some furniture. The name of the place was Ain Charod, and while Chayim was putting down the furniture, Avram walked with Daavid and showed him a stream that ran through the land. It was the stream of Charod, after which the settlement was named.

"It was by this stream that Gideon chose his raiders," Avram said.

"How did he choose them?" Daavid asked.

"By the way they drank from the stream," Avram said. The stream was narrow and fast, and the water was clean. Daavid was thirsty too, and ready to drink.

"Let me see how you will drink," Avram said with his half-serious smile.

Daavid knelt, scooped up water in his hands, and drank it.

"That's good," Avram said. "You could be one of Gideon's men, one of the three hundred."

"Then how did the others drink?" Daavid asked, "the ones that were not chosen?"

"They lay down and drank from the stream with their faces," Avram told him. "You are an old partisan, so surely you know why that is bad?"

"Because anyone could come up behind them and kill them," Daavid said. Avram nodded seriously, and Daavid knew that Avram had really meant it, then, that he had passed the test to be a man of Gideon.

They went on their way again, and Chayim drove past a hill that was dug out like a mine. The name of this place was Megiddo, a place of many battles, Avram said, and the digging was an excavation, where the remains of all the battles have been found, one under the other.

"Did they find the bones of the Turks?" Daavid asked.

"Yes," Avram said.

"And of the Romans, under them?"

"Romans too," Avram said.

"And of the Greeks?"

"Yes," Avram said, "and beneath them were the bones of the Philistines, and beneath them were the Egyptians."

Then Daavid began to laugh.

"Why are you laughing?" Miriam asked.

But Avram did not have to be told.

They came to factories, and to a great city, and they drove up the mountain, Mount Carmel, and they saw the whole city lying below them by the sea, and David felt surely that in all this where there was so much life, his people lived.

Chayim stopped the truck in front of a café on Mount Carmel. It was high up on the side of the mountain, overlooking the city, and from the steps of the café they could see the entire harbor, with ships and warships lying against the city. A little way inland they could see two great structures, like immense coffeepots, with smoke coming from them. These were oil refineries, Avram said, to which oil came in a pipe, from all the way across Palestine, and here it was turned into gasoline, to be put into the English warships in order to make them go. "And that is why the English are here," he said.

"*Shalom,* Avram," the waiter said. He looked at Daavid. "Immigration? From the other night?" The waiter winked.

"You know everything, Ben-Shmuel!" Avram said. The waiter was a thin man with a long face, and one shoulder higher than the other, as though he were always holding up a tray.

Avram wanted them to wait there while he went to buy some DDT.

"No DDT has arrived yet," the waiter said. He knew everything.

But Avram said, "Don't worry, Ben-Shmuel."

"Tea and cakes?" the waiter asked them.

"Just tea," Miriam said.

"Cakes too," Avram ordered, and left them.

"And for you, comrade?" the waiter asked Daavid. "Ice cream?"

"What's that?" Daavid asked. From where he sat he could see a ship, far out in the water, coming toward the harbor.

The waiter explained that ice cream was an American invention. He talked very fast and he liked to talk. "Surely, like all of us in Palestine," he said to Daavid, "you have a rich uncle in America? Well, he makes ice cream."

Daavid thought it was some kind of a joke about the uncle, but to make sure he said, "I have my whole family here in Palestine."

"A lucky family," the waiter said. "Where do you live in Palestine?"

"He is going to live in the children's colony," Miriam told the waiter.

"Until I find my family," Daavid added.

The waiter looked at him the way he had looked at Avram, with his eyes narrowed, like an expert seeing through everybody and knowing everything. "You'll find them," he declared. "In our little country everybody finds what he seeks." And he went away.

Now, sitting alone with Miriam, Daavid felt strange. He could not look directly into her face, but looked out at the water, watching the ship, wondering if it was a British military ship coming to get some of the oil, or bringing more soldiers, and then he looked around at the people at the other tables. He knew Miriam wanted to say something to him now, because they might not see each other any more. She wanted to say something, perhaps like a mother, only she could never really be like a mother. And sometimes he nearly hated her because she didn't believe in his mother and father. If only Miriam would believe in them, then he would know for sure.

Now she began to talk to him, but he thought it still was not truly what she needed to tell him. At the children's village, she said, he would have new friends, boys just like himself. And he would learn things, he would learn to read and write.

"I never had a letter just for myself," he told her.

"I'll write to you," Miriam said, "and after you learn, you can write to me."

Perhaps it was only because she had never seen his family that she didn't really believe in them. And now that he was leaving her, Daavid wanted to make Miriam know, in some way he had to make her believe in them. He asked Miriam for a piece of paper and pencil and began to draw a picture.

The waiter brought the ice cream. It was something cold and smooth and tasted sweet; it was one of the good things of the world. "Did it come all the way from America?" Daavid asked. "On a ship?"

No, the waiter said, it was an American invention, but it was made right here in Haifa, as good as in America. Where did he come from, the waiter wanted to know, from Birkenau, from Dachau, from Belsen?

From Buchenwald, Daavid said, and he went on with his drawing, because the ice cream was too good to eat all at once.

"Eat! Eat ice cream!" The waiter moved the dish even closer to Daavid and then hurried away.

Miriam began again, after the waiter was gone, and this time Daavid knew she was saying what was important to her. "Daavid," she said, "sometimes a boy needs someone special to do things for him. If people don't understand you, or if there is anything you want—ask for me, for Miriam, who came with you to Palestine. Yes?"

"All right," he said.

She leaned over and looked at what he was doing. "What are you drawing, Daavid?"

He showed her. He was drawing his mother and father. "That is so if they come looking for me, you'll know them," he explained. "You can tell them where I am."

"Yes," Miriam said, "I'll always know where you are."

He drew his mother's hair, long, all around her shoulders.

"What lovely long hair your mother had," Miriam said.

Then after a moment she opened her purse and took something out of it. "Listen, Daavid," Miriam said, "I want to give you a present." She said the present had to be a secret between the two of them. He asked if he could tell Avram, and Miriam said no, he must not even tell Avram. Then she gave him the present.

It was the size of a jackknife, with a smooth shell cover, but instead of a knifeblade, a comb opened out of it. "I know boys don't like to comb their hair very much," Miriam said, smiling the secret way she did sometimes over something between them, "but I wanted you to have this because it is the only thing I've had all this time. It is really a man's comb," she said. "A man gave it to me a long time ago. It's the only thing they let me keep."

Daavid opened and shut the comb, like a knife. But they had cut off all the ladies' hair, he remembered. Sometimes he had had dreams, bad dreams about it, about his mother, and they were cutting off her hair.

"They cut off all the ladies' hair," he said to Miriam. "Why did they let you keep this?" Then he knew he should not have said that. Miriam didn't answer him right away. Maybe there was something so bad even he didn't know how bad it was.

"Some of us had to keep our hair," Miriam said at last. "So they let me keep this comb."

"Your hair is nice," Daavid said. He opened the comb and passed it through his hair.

"After you have learned a great deal at the school," Miriam said, "you will come back and live with us at Makor Gallil."

"I'll be with my family," he reminded her.

She looked at him and smiled the small secret smile that was between them. Maybe, maybe now she believed.

He went on with his drawing. He drew uncles and aunts and a brother.

Avram came back, and Avram knew right away that the picture was Daavid's family. Daavid showed him his mother and father and cousins and uncles. He told Avram names for them. "Uncle Zalman and Aunt Sophie and Aunt Leah and—"

"What about grandfathers?" Avram said.

Daavid put in two grandfathers, one with a beard and one with no hair on his head. Miriam was silent again, as if she were not there. Perhaps, because of their secret from Avram.

"And you?" Avram said. "Aren't you in the family picture?"

So Daavid put himself in, between his father and mother. The picture was finished. He decided to give it to Miriam. Though he really wanted to keep his family, still he felt satisfied to give it to her. That must have been the way she had felt, giving him the comb.

"This is a present for you, Miriam," Daavid said, "so if anyone of my family comes, you'll know them."

"Thank you, Daavid," she said. She smiled, even though Avram was there. He was glad he had given it to her. Now she knew and surely believed.

The waiter had returned. "Well, Avram. Did you get the DDT?" he asked.

"Did you think I wouldn't?" Avram said.

It was like an old joke between them.

Then the waiter looked at the drawing in Miriam's hand. "What a fine family," he said to Daavid.

And suddenly a thought came to Daavid. Surely the waiter saw many people every day.

"I see everybody in Palestine," the waiter declared.

"Maybe somebody from my family will come in here," Daavid said. "Tell them Miriam knows where I am."

"I'll watch for them!" the waiter promised. "And after all," he said, "such things really do happen. I've seen such a miracle, right where you are sitting! Right here at this table a brother met his sister! Every time a new ship came into port, a legal ship, from immigration A, the brother came to look for his sister. And last month, on the *Transylvania,* she was there! They met! He brought her right here, to my table!" The waiter studied Daavid with his narrowed, expert eyes. "Who knows, perhaps you will even meet someone on the ship today!"

A ship? Daavid looked at the port below. The vessel was already through the opening, and in the harbor. Then it was not a warship, but a ship bringing people!

It was this month's quota, the waiter said. Surely they had come to meet it.

Daavid looked at Avram and Miriam.

"I suppose now we must go," Miriam said to Avram.

The boat was right there, in the harbor. As the truck turned into a short street that led to the harbor, they could see it. The boat seemed to be right at the end of the street. They could even see people, quite small, pressed against the ship's railings, waving their arms. But there was a barrier at the entrance to the harbor, and police were standing there, and there was also an armored car with soldiers, to keep people from going into the harbor to meet their relatives. A large crowd pressed close against the barrier, waiting.

When the truck reached the barrier a policeman stopped it; but a second policeman, a Jew, came over on the other side.

98

Avram leaned over to him, and the policeman said *"Shalom, Avram."* Everybody everywhere knew Avram.

"We're going to pick up some DDT that came from America," Avram said.

The second policeman said the truck could go into the harbor. The barrier was lifted and Chayim drove through.

Daavid stared at the ship. It was a regular ship, four times as large as the *Hannah Szenesch,* and people were coming from it, into Palestine, in the daylight. Out of all the hundreds of thousands who were waiting in the camps, Avram explained, a few were permitted to come legally, like this, in the daylight.

"They are some of the people who have papers from their families that are already in Palestine," he said.

Daavid watched them as they came down from the ship. There was a very old blind man, and a soldier ran halfway up to meet him; the soldier had the same blue and white insignia as Avram's on his sleeve. Word spread quickly among the few people who had managed to come to the side of the ship—the soldier was the blind man's son.

Then came more old people, and one was carrying a large scroll wrapped in blue velvet, with a star sewn on it, and he was carrying it in his arms like a baby. This was a scroll of the holy law, Avram said, that the grandfather had perhaps hidden in the ground, and at last he had saved it out of Europe. Then came a whole family together, a mother and father and a boy, smaller than Daavid; the mother carried a baby in her arms, wrapped in a blanket, and the boy was only as big as Daavid had been in Poland. Then came more people, of all ages, and Daavid watched them carefully, looking into each face, wondering if any of them could be his family.

It was as though he were trying to recognize someone in the dark, for he could not bring faces sharply to his mind; it was as though he remembered by shapes leaning over his bed when the lights were put out and he was going to sleep. Then he saw a tall man coming down from the ship. The man carried his hat so that his head was bare; his hair was a little thin. The man was alone, and no one met him, and he looked around as though to find someone.

Daavid felt that he had to ask. Because if he did not ask, and

99

by one chance in a million this man was his father, he would not know how to find him again, and then the chance would have been lost forever.

He went up to the man and said, "My name is Daavid Halevi." The man looked at him carefully.

"I thought perhaps—" and Daavid waited for the man to respond. Then he added, "I'm looking for my father."

Slowly the man shook his head. "No," he said. "No." And still he looked at Daavid. "But my boy would have been your age by now," he said. Then he went away.

Another woman carrying a baby came from the ship, and Daavid saw a man break wildly through the barrier and run toward them while the police yelled after him. The woman ran toward him, and the baby was laughing and laughing as they came together, hugging the baby between them. All around people were meeting and hugging each other. There were even children coming from the ship, and mothers and fathers ran to them and seized them, lifting them up off the ground and hugging them, hugging them.

Daavid went back toward the truck. He didn't want anyone to come near him. Miriam came near. He didn't want her to say anything, he wished she wouldn't, he withdrew within himself.

"You know, Daavid," she said, "many people lose their parents when they are children. They grow up, the same as other people. Not only the children in Europe lost their mothers and fathers," Miriam told him. "Sometimes it happens in other ways than wars. You know Avram lost his mother here in Palestine."

Then she didn't believe at all! She didn't even want to believe! Just as he had always known within himself, Miriam was against him.

Daavid turned and faced her. "You don't care if I find my father and mother," he said. "You don't even want them to be alive."

He felt the same as one time when he had hit a boy who was his friend, and been sorry, but had gone on hitting the boy even harder, as though against his own self. "Give me back my picture," he demanded.

100

Miriam took the drawing from her purse and handed it to him.

Daavid started to give her back the comb, but she closed her hand over his and would not take back the present. She walked to the front of the truck.

Avram was still standing near him. "You're wrong, Daavid," Avram said. "Miriam cares very much. She wanted them to be alive."

Daavid and Avram climbed into the back of the truck, where they had boxes to sit on. Then they drove out through the city, and along the sea, passing a big British army camp and a place where there were great fields filled with army trucks and jeeps and tanks.

And then suddenly they came to a concentration camp. It was on the right side of the road. It was exactly the same as in Europe, with barbed wire and a tower, where he could see soldiers and machine guns, and there was a gate, with guards and pillboxes and machine-gun slits, and inside there were rows of barracks. The truck stopped. For a moment a terrible panic came over Daavid, a fear that they were bringing him here to give him over to this place. For even they, even Miriam, even Avram, how could he know what they would do with him? They were not his own family.

But it was soldiers who had stopped the truck. Two soldiers came and put tommy guns against them and made them all get out of the truck. The soldiers asked for papers. The three grown people handed theirs over, and the soldiers looked at Daavid for a moment, but did not ask for his papers, because he was still a child. Everyone was silent while the soldiers examined Miriam's card. It was a false one, Daavid knew. The soldiers looked at her face, and then they gave the paper back to her, and she put it carefully into her purse. Avram and Chayim also put away their identity cards. The soldiers picked up the seat of the truck and looked under it; then they picked up Daavid's pack. "What's in the sack?" one of them asked. "Clothes," Avram said. The soldier opened the sack, felt in it with his hand, then gave it back to Daavid. The other soldier climbed into the back of the truck, looked, and came down. Then the soldiers motioned with their guns for them to get back into the vehicle, letting them go on their way.

Daavid breathed very shallowly until they were well beyond the concentration camp.

They passed olive groves, and on the left there were caves again in the side of the mountain. These were not fighters' caves, Avram said, but prehistoric caves. In these caves bones had been found of men who had lived a hundred thousand years ago. Daavid asked if they were Jews, too, and if they had been killed fighting to the last man, and Avram laughed. No, Avram said, these caves were there before men knew they were Jews or British or Greeks, and at that time they probably fought the animals as much as each other.

Then they reached a cultivated place, which Avram said was the farm of the children's village. But the village itself was up on top of the mountain. The truck snaked up the mountain. The children's village looked the same as any settlement, with large houses, though Daavid had pictured the houses as child-size. They could look far out to sea from the top of the mountain.

The truck halted in front of a building that had a porch with wide stairs. Several children were sitting on the stairs, and as the truck stopped a woman came from the building. As soon as she saw them, she called, *"Shalom,* Avram!"

"Shalom, Malka," he said.

She was a small woman, with a very soft face, and when they told her Daavid's name she said, *"Shalom,* Daavid," and didn't look at him too much. But she saw the air force emblem on his jacket and said there were some more boys from Europe who belonged to the same air force. She said half the day he would work in the shops or in the garden, learning how to do things, and half the day he would study in the school. She showed him where the school was—a white building behind a playing field.

Some boys were crossing the yard in a wagon, and Malka called to them, "Yaakov, is that for the bull?" The boy called back, "Yes," and she said they were driving to the bullpen, and Daavid could go with them to help feed the bull.

"Here's another paratrooper," she called to the boys; "Daavid Halévi."

102

Miriam and Avram said *shalom* to him, and he went and climbed up on the wagon.

The boys were mostly his own size, though the one who was driving was bigger. All except one of the boys had numbers on their arms.

The one whom Malka had called Yaakov had cropped hair, like in Europe. He was sitting on a sack, and he made room for Daavid. He had a large chest and strong-looking hands with big knuckles.

"Is that your real name?" Daavid asked. "Yaakov?"

"Sure it's my name," Yaakov said.

Daavid didn't feel anything against him, but he said, "I bet they just gave you a name here in Palestine, and it isn't even what your name was at home."

Yaakov said, "I don't know what my name was at home. I was too little. The SS only called me *Schmutz*—Dirty."

Daavid said, "I have my own real name. I wouldn't let anybody change it. I even have my own family name, Halevi."

The dark boy that didn't have any numbers was like the Yemenite girl that had been at the settlement. Now he proclaimed, "My name is like it always was, Aryay Yedidi."

"You haven't even got a number," Daavid said.

Yaakov explained that Aryay had not been in a camp. He had come from Tripoli, a place in Africa, not Europe. "We call him the Arab," he said.

Then why had the boy come here? Daavid wondered. "Why didn't you stay home with your family if they didn't put you in camps?" he asked.

"They killed my family," Aryay said. "It was a pogrom. The Arabs came into our house and killed everybody."

Then Yaakov said, "In our village the Germans drove everybody into the synagogue and burned everybody. It was the biggest fire you ever saw."

The boy who was sitting with the mule-driver turned and said, "In our town they couldn't even get everybody into the synagogue. They burned whole streets."

"We had a big synagogue," Yaakov declared.

Daavid told them, "We lived in a city. They made everybody

103

come into the big square. Thousands and thousands of people. And they mowed them down with machine guns."

They had come to the bullpen, and they jumped off the wagon and began emptying the sacks over the strong iron railing into the pen. The bull was huge and strong enough to do anything.

The largest boy, Baruch, who had been driving the mules, turned to Daavid and said, "You didn't see anything. In Auschwitz they gave me the job of carrying the gas cylinders to the crematorium. Every day I saw them burning up thousands and thousands of people. Just the ashes alone would fill your whole city square."

They all watched the bull devouring the corn.

"I bet he can break loose if he wants to," Daavid said.

He was in the same room with Yaakov and the dark-skinned Aryay. The room held all kinds of things the boys had picked up, an iron spearhead, old stones they had found on the mountainside with the prints of seashells in them, and Yaakov said that proved that even before people had lived in the caves the sea had come up to the top of the mountain. But Aryay said no, it proved that it was true what the Bible said about Noah, that there was a deluge of rain, and that it rained until the whole world was covered up, and everybody was drowned because they were bad people.

"Who was Noah?" Daavid asked.

Yaakov was lying on his bed, scratching his skull and watching Daavid as he opened his sack and put away his things. "Noah was a forefather, a father of the fathers of Avraham," he said.

"And who was Avraham?"

"Avraham," Aryay said, "was the father of all Israel."

"What about Adam?" Yaakov demanded. "He was even before, because he was the first man."

"Well, then Avraham was the first Jew," Aryay said, "because he was the first one to come to Eretz Yisroel."

There were other things in the room, dried seeds, and the skull of a sheep, and there were even pictures on the wall. Daavid stood and looked at a photograph of a man and a woman. They were both smiling, and they were not too old. "Who are they?" Daavid asked Yaakov.

"That's my family in America," Yaakov said.

"Then if you have a family, why don't you go there and live with them?" Daavid asked.

The fourth boy that lived in the room, Shlomo, came in from washing and flung his towel on his bed. "That's not his real family," Shlomo explained. "That's just some people in America that write letters and send us things."

"They even sent me this fountain pen, because I write the letters," Yaakov said. He took the pen from under his pillow, where he kept it at night, and held it up for Daavid to see.

"They sent us their picture and they want us to send them our picture," said Shlomo. He sucked in his lips as he laughed. "They are even going to send us a camera to take pictures. Wait till they see Yaakov's face with his pig-nose, they'll stop altogether!" He snapped his towel at Yaakov, and Yaakov half rose to make a lunge at him.

"We'll tell them we have a new comrade," Aryay suggested. "Their hearts will melt with pity and they'll send us some more things. What should we ask them for?"

"They call us their three little sons," Shlomo said. "So we'll tell them they've got another little son."

"They even say they are coming here to see us some day," Yaakov said. "As soon as the British give them a visa."

"You can write to them yourself," Aryay offered. "Their name is Rabinowitch. In Saint Louis. That's in the middle of America. Only everything you get you have to divide."

Daavid took his own picture out of his pocket and unfolded it. "Where is a hammer and a nail?" he asked.

There was a little box with some nails and bits of things, and he found a small bent nail and picked up the spearhead to use as a hammer.

"That's mine!" Shlomo cried, but then relented. "All right, you can use it."

Daavid spread the drawing on the wall over his head and began to tack it. Shlomo stood behind him to watch him use the spearhead.

"This is my own real family," Daavid said.

"That's just a picture you drew yourself," declared Shlomo.

"It's my father and mother and my whole family," Daavid insisted. "You'll see. They'll come for me."

Aryay came closer to look at the drawing. "We don't have fathers and mothers," he said. "All of our families were killed."

"Not mine!" Daavid told them. A whole event came into his mind, as clearly as though he had lived through it. "When they were in the train, my father knocked over the SS and took my mother and they jumped from the train with my baby sisters, and that's how they came to Palestine."

Yaakov had risen from his bed. "You made it all up," he declared.

"You'll see! You'll see!" Daavid cried out. "They'll come for me. Tomorrow!"

"They'll never come for you," Yaakov shouted angrily. "They're dead, just like ours."

Shlomo laughed, sucking in his lips.

"They'll come, they'll come!" Daavid cried.

Yaakov gripped him by the shoulders and yelled at him fiercely. He had small sharp teeth, like a baby's, separated by gaps. "Why do you think you're here if you've got a mother and father?"

"This place is only for orphans!" Aryay shouted.

Their faces were all around him, on every side, shouting at him as though he had attacked them all.

"You're just like the rest of us!" Yaakov cried hotly, and at the same moment Daavid saw Shlomo reach and pull the drawing off the wall, still laughing his dirty sucked-in laugh.

"No! No! Give me that!" He leaped at Shlomo. Shlomo tore away from him, waving the piece of paper, and Daavid lunged after him, catching hold of his pajama shirt. He pulled and grabbed, and Shlomo came down on top of him. They fell on a cot, and rolled off, fighting, falling on the floor. Daavid felt his head bump on a chair leg, but that didn't matter. He clawed, trying to get at the hand that held the drawing, but it was just out of reach, almost on the floor among the feet of the other boys, and at any moment they would trample his picture.

He caught hold of Shlomo's hair and pounded the boy's head on the floor, shouting, "Give it to me! Give it to me!" Then Yaakov was on top of him, and he fought them both, not caring how strong Yaakov was. He saw his chance and let go of Shlomo's head and tore at his hand, almost reaching the picture, but just then Aryay's dark hand reached down and snatched it, and then Aryay jumped away.

He would kill them all! Kill them all! Daavid leaped, breaking the hold Yaakov had on him and throwing him off. Somehow, in rising, he seized the spearhead and would have smashed Aryay's brains with it.

But just then a big fellow came rushing into the room and took hold of both Daavid and Aryay by their shoulders, pulling them apart. He was twice as big as they were, and he had a grip with his fist like an SS.

"They took my picture!" Daavid said. And even under the grip he lunged for the drawing. "Give it to me!"

"I was only holding it for you," Aryay said and handed it back to him.

Daavid uncrumpled the sheet of paper. It was torn.

They went to their beds. The monitor put out the light.

He could have no friends. Even Maccabee had left him, and Miriam did not believe, and Avram had let them send him here, as though he were an orphan. Here they were his enemies. They wanted to take everything away from him, even his family.

He would be alone in the world until he found his own people. Then everybody would know, then everybody would see that they had been wrong. He would come with his father and mother to this place and show his parents to Malka, and she would be very respectful to them and walk with them all around the place to show them how nice she had made things for their boy, and he would show his parents to Yaakov and Shlomo and Aryay right in this room, and he would not tell about the fight because it would be revenge enough when these boys saw his tall father and his mother, so nicely dressed.

The way to go, Daavid decided, would be to pick up his clothes and sandals and all of his things and go to the washroom. He could put the light on there and dress.

He took the drawing from under his pillow, folded it carefully in the darkness, and placed it in his sack. Soundlessly he gathered his clothes. It was easy to leave the school. He prepared himself as he had planned and then slipped out of the house, by the door. He kept away from the open yard and stayed behind trees until he came to the edge of the grounds. There was a fence, but he was sure it was not electrified, and he had only to slip under the wire.

Chapter Six

Outside of the grounds there were no more trees, but only rocks on the mountainside. Daavid clambered hurriedly, to get far enough away from the place so that they could not find him. In the morning he would look for the main road.

There was a noise that came from behind and all around him. It was a howl and a whine together, and it seemed to come from every rock. In the forests, in Poland, he had heard the wolves, and he had been very small and had been terrified. This was nearer, but it was not the sound of wolves.

He knew what it was now. He had heard it that night at the settlement when he had walked back from the river with Miriam. It was jackals, Miriam had said. Only then they had not sounded so near.

He had not seen one. But it was a sound unlike an animal; it was as though it came out of the earth, and everywhere, even in itself, was fright and pain.

But there was no need to be afraid of them. A jackal was afraid of a man.

Daavid ran, clambering with his hands and his feet among the rocks. Again and again he hurt his feet and his ankles against stones. He would find a cave, one of the caves where people had lived a hundred thousand years ago, and where the Maccabees had held out and fought the invaders.

He climbed over huge rocks, and then there was a small flat place, in among the rocks, open only on one side. Daavid went carefully as far as he could on the open side, for one had always to examine the ways that were open to attack. The open part was a ledge, and there the mountain fell away into darkness. He could see nothing below, only the darkness—perhaps the sea was below, or the end of the world and nothingness.

Daavid drew back against the big rocks, to something that he could feel. He found a crevice and prepared to lie down. The wailing of the jackals was all around him, and it seemed to come even out of the bottomless blackness.

There were loose stones on the ground. He gathered them and made a pile to keep by his side, within reach of his hand. Then he tried to go to sleep. But as he curled against the rock the howling came again, and he remembered the skull in the boys' room, the rows of teeth, and a wave of anguish, of utter loneliness, swept through him, and he pressed himself against the rock as though it were a warm body to embrace him, and he spoke a word that came and came within him, as though surely now it would bring, it had to bring, an answer.

"Papa . . . Papa."

Then Daavid dreamed, and knew he was dreaming, and in the dream he went into a cave, an ancient cave such as those that Avram had shown him, within these mountains. Far back within the cave, against the curved wall, his father and mother sat. There was a warm red glow on them, and upon the walls of the cave, and his mother held a very small child in her lap, and the child was himself, Daavid.

And in his dream, which he knew was a dream, he saw his mother, exactly as she was, and he told himself that now that he knew exactly how she looked, he would be able to find her, and he must remember how she looked, so that he would know when he awakened.

Then a darkness came upon the cave, and they had to flee. His father placed him in a sack, and took his mother by the hand, and they began to flee. They fled over the dark depth of nothingness that was just outside the cave, and over the dark water, and he was curled in the sack, so that no one would find him. He was carried thus to the gates of the camp, and there soldiers stood, with fixed bayonets. There was a long line of people, and his father was in the line, carrying him, and as the line of people came to the soldiers, each one had to open his sack and show what was there. Sometimes the soldiers only jabbed their bayonets through a man's sack, and Daavid waited, fearing that this would happen. He curled himself smaller and smaller within the sack, and feared that they would open it, and drag him out, and feared that their knives would rip it and pierce into him.

They were tearing at the outside of the sack.

And Daavid knew he was dreaming and that the jackals had surely come and were tearing his clothes with their teeth.

He awakened, and it was day, and only a goat with black whiskers was tugging at his jacket, and around him were other goats, black ones and white ones, and above him on the rock an Arab herdsman leaned, calling to him.

Daavid arose and saw where he had come in the night. Far below was the sea, and along its shore he saw a road, with cars. He climbed out to the Arab, who looked at him curiously and said, "*Marhaba.*"

Daavid replied with the word that Mustafa had taught him, "*Marhabtein.*"

The Arab continued to gaze at him, and then drew a round piece of Arab bread from under his cloak, broke off a piece, and held it out to Daavid. Daavid accepted the bread and smiled, saying, "*Shalom.*"

The Arab said, "*Shalom,*" and Daavid went down the side of the mountain toward the sea. He ate the bread, and on the way he stopped and picked up a few little stones, with the print of seashells on them; he put them in his pocket. Below, there were several black tents, and a few Arab shepherds with flocks. He passed them and reached the road.

He stood on the road, not knowing which way to go. A few trucks passed, but did not stop for him. Then a young Arab from the black tents came down to the road with his flock of sheep and led them across the road, and while the sheep were crossing, automobiles had to stop. Daavid went up to a car that seemed to have plenty of room, since only two men were in it, and the back seat was empty. But as he reached it he feared he had made a mistake, for the men were not Jews. The one who was driving wore a fez, a red Arab hat, though he was otherwise dressed like a European; and the one who sat next to him was very large, with a smooth face, and was surely an Englishman.

The Englishman spoke to him in Hebrew. "What is it? What is it, boy?" he said.

"I come from school, and have to go to my father," Daavid said.

The Arab studied him and remarked, "Looks like he has been fighting," and Daavid remembered the scratches and bruises on his face.

"Got in a fight, and running away from school, is that it?" the Englishman said.

Since this seemed to please the man, Daavid said, "Yes."

All the sheep were by now across the road, and the trucks were starting. The Arab put the car into gear; Daavid heard it.

"Well, hop in," the Englishman said, opening the door to the back of the car. "I suppose a Jew who runs away from school ought to be encouraged."

Daavid quickly got in as the car began to move.

"What did you do to the other fellow?" the Englishman called back to him. "Beat him up?"

"There were three other fellows," Daavid said.

Again he had said the right thing, for the Englishman was satisfied. "There are always three other fellows!" he said. "What's your name, boy?"

Daavid told them. "Halevi. Daavid."

At this the Arab turned his head around and looked at him carefully. "Halevi?" the Arab repeated. "The violinist? Is he your father?"

Suddenly Daavid knew that everything he had done, running away from the school and going on his search, had been exactly right. "Yes! my father plays the violin!" he said.

The Arab turned to the Englishman. "But I have heard his father many times. Halevi is the first violinist of their symphony orchestra."

The Englishman said he did not care for symphony orchestras, he preferred the films.

Then the Arab asked Daavid, "Do you play the violin, too?"

Daavid had the flute that he had made with Mustafa. "I am learning to play on this," he said, taking it out of his sack.

And again he had pleased the Englishman, who said, "That's more like it. You people may learn to live in this country yet."

Daavid tried to play the little tune that Mustafa had taught him.

It was a warm day, and they went very fast in their car, passing all the trucks on the road and even passing a whole convoy of armored cars and jeeps and motorcycles. These men were very important, he was certain. After a while the men were finished being amused with him and sat talking to each other, and he felt easier, and sat and watched the places by the road. Here there was no wilderness; there were fields, and there were groves of trees, and many Palestinians.

Then the car came to a city. It appeared suddenly, with its tall white apartment buildings, and the road became a street, which was filled with automobiles and carts and men and women on bicycles, so that the car had to go very slowly. It was much busier and more crowded than Haifa, where he had been with Avram and Miriam. It was surely the city of Tel Aviv of which everybody talked. This street was like the streets in America, that American soldiers had told him about.

Once when the car had to wait at a crossing the Englishman turned and said, "Where do you live, son? Where do you want to go?"

Daavid was startled, fearing that they might find him out now. But he said, "I want to go to my father—Mr. Halevi, the violinist."

The Englishman said, "That's right. Always better to see your father first if you've been fighting. Always followed that policy myself."

The car made another turn and then halted in front of a huge building with glass doors and signs on it. The Arab said his father's orchestra was probably in there now. And as Daavid got out of the car, the Arab said, "Give your father the compliments of Hassan Effendi, of the Government Department of Antiquities."

Daavid thanked them and said, *"Shalom!"*

They replied, *"Shalom,"* and smiled to each other, and drove away.

Daavid tried to open one of the big doors of the building. It was locked. But he knew that there were people inside, for he could hear, faintly, the sound of music. He tried another door, and it was open.

This was a theater, he knew. It was the first time he had been inside of such a place. Daavid walked carefully. No one was in the hallway. On the walls were pictures of people in strange clothes; some were dressed like Arabs. He could hear the music a little more strongly now. It was like music he had heard sometimes on the radio, when everything played together, violins and pianos and drums and every kind of instrument.

There was another row of doors, and the first of these was unlocked, and as he opened the door the music struck him so that he nearly let go of the door. The music was like a thousand airplanes in the air.

There was an immense hall in front of him, with rows of seats, but all the seats were empty. Then there was the stage. The stage was filled with musicians, sitting on chairs, and in the center, in front of them, stood a leader who was drawing in the air with his hands and his arms, the sounds of the music.

Daavid made his way slowly between the rows of seats, coming closer to the musicians. Almost all of them were men, though there were three or four ladies too. On each side of the leader were rows of musicians playing violins. Behind them were musicians playing other instruments, and one played a big violin that stood on the floor.

Daavid came to the very edge of the stage, and he looked up at their faces. They did not notice him, they were entirely in their music, and he pressed along the edge of the stage, looking from one to the other of them. He was afraid to choose which it might be. Some of them were young, and some of them were gray and even fat, like uncles. One of them wore glasses and had a bald head. But even if it were he, Daavid thought, he would be glad. And it was strange, because while they were playing the music all their faces were good. He was not afraid of any of them.

The music became softer now, and he did not move. For a moment some of the violins did not play; the men rested, holding their violins, waiting until their turn came again, and one of these men who was resting looked down toward Daavid with a small, understanding smile. Now, it would be now. Daavid felt it must surely happen! His father would know him and reach out to him. Then the man put his violin under his chin and began to play again.

The music was like a field of grass. He waited, almost smiling. They played on and on. Everything in him beat fast, racing with the music.

There was a small stairway at the end of the stage, and while the music was loud Daavid slipped noiselessly to this stairway, and climbed up, and stood at the end of the stage, near the stout man who held the big fiddle, fat like himself, that stood on the floor.

A little dark hollow-faced man in a sweater was sitting there, with pages of music on his lap.

"Halevi," Daavid whispered to him. "Which one is Halevi?"

The man put his finger to his lips. Daavid froze, motionless.

Just then the leader rapped with his stick. The music broke, teetered for an instant, and came to a halt. Leaning far over his desk, the leader began talking to one of the musicians, and the man became excited and ran up to him with a page of music, and they bent over the page, arguing.

The man in the sweater, near David, took his finger from his lips. "What do you want, boy?" he said.

Daavid asked, "Which one is Halevi?"

"What do you want Halevi for?"

Daavid could not answer. For it was already like the beginning of a defeat. If they didn't know at once, if they didn't see—

"Did someone send you?" the man kept questioning him. And Daavid began to feel wrong, and foolish, and wanted to turn and run away. Because of the music, a picture had grown in his mind: they would see him and cry out, "This is Halevi's boy Daavid! He has been seeking him everywhere!" And the violinist would come toward him, and the music—

But now the fat man with the fat standing fiddle repeated the name, calling, "Halevi, someone wants you!" And a man in the midst of the musicians close to the leader turned around in his chair and then arose.

He was tall, and had a good strong face.

Yes, yes, Daavid thought. It must be he.

His sleeves were rolled up and his arms were sinewy; his hands were strong. Holding his violin, the man came between the players, toward him, and leaned down a little, smiling seriously. "Did you want me?" he asked.

"Yes," Daavid said. "If you are—" He did not dare say more. Why didn't the man know him? Why didn't he know at once and help? "I'm Daavid," he whispered. "Daavid."

The man leaned still lower and touched him, placing his free hand on Daavid's shoulder. "And what do you want of me, Daavid?" he asked.

Nothing would come any more, and in a moment he might cry.

The leader's rapping sounded, he was rapping on his desk, and the violinist glanced back toward the leader, but did not leave Daavid.

The first one, in the sweater, said, "This is a rehearsal, boy. Every minute costs five pounds. You'll have to go."

Just then the violinist dropped his arm from Daavid's shoulder and touched his wrist, where the numbers were. "You're a survivor," he said. "From Auschwitz."

Daavid looked him fully in the face. Surely it would come now.

The leader rapped again and held his arms in the air. The musician who had been arguing there was finished and was returning to his chair. The leader looked over at them. He called to the man in the sweater. "Pinchas, what is it?"

Pinchas waved his hands at Daavid and the violinist Halevi.

"Can we wait a moment?" Halevi called. And someone in between whispered up to the leader what was happening.

It was his last moment then. Daavid looked the violinist fully in the face. "Don't you know me?" he asked. "I came to find the family—isn't it you?" Still nothing changed in the man. And now Daavid felt all of the musicians leaning in on him, all of them trying to help him bring his wish through.

"I?" the man said.

"Halevi," Daavid repeated. "And my father played the violin."

"What was his name?" the man asked strangely.

"Our name. Halevi."

Even the leader had come down from his stand and was coming toward them.

"I understand, I understand!" the man in the sweater, Pinchas, explained. "The boy is looking for his father, whose name is Halevi." Triumphantly he demanded of Daavid, "Isn't it so?"

If only all the others weren't there, Daavid felt, if it were only between the two of them, himself and the violinist, it would be easier. "Don't you come from Poland? From Cracow?" he asked.

Slowly the man shook his head. "I come from Rumania," he said.

The leader said, "We come from every country, child."

And then, as though the two of them were after all alone, the violinist knelt until he was no taller than Daavid. "Daavid, I wish it had been so," he said. "A boy like you. But I have no children."

The leader was going to go back to his stand, and the violinist would have to go back to his chair. Now, Daavid knew, he had to go away.

"Wait! I met a Halevi," Pinchas cried. "From Poland!" His eyes sparkled, and the words rushed out of him. "He came a few years ago, he escaped. His name was Yehuda Halevi—I remember exactly, because it is the same name as the poet, Yehuda Halevi. Is that your father?" he demanded.

"He escaped?" Daavid repeated. "From Poland?"

"Wait! I know where he is!" The musicians were crowding around again, and Pinchas spoke in triumph to them all. "He is at the potash works, near the Dead Sea! Yes, I remember exactly, because he said I could see the potash works if I came to visit him!"

"Is it far?" Daavid asked.

The leader had stopped to listen. He studied Daavid, and asked, "You said your father played the violin?"

The fat man with the big fiddle said, "Well, who knows what a man did in Poland, and what he does in Palestine."

"How can I go there?" Daavid asked.

"To the Dead Sea? In an autobus, from the big station," the leader said, and went back to his place, as if everything were satisfactorily finished. He tapped again on his stand, and the musicians began to return to their chairs and settle down to their music.

Halevi lingered, the last to leave him. "You're not going by yourself? Who takes care of you, Daavid? Where do you live?"

"The school," Daavid said quickly. "I live in a school."

The tapping came again. Pinchas touched Halevi impatiently. Hastily Halevi took something from his pocket and handed it to Daavid. It was money.

"Buy yourself some ice cream, Daavid," he said, smiling, and started back to his chair.

Daavid felt much easier now. "Thank you," he said. "I like ice cream."

They were playing as he went out, and Halevi caught his eye and smiled to him, bending harder into his music, playing, as if saying something cheerful to Daavid.

In the street Daavid asked a big boy, who was standing with a bicycle, which was the way to the station where there was the autobus to the Dead Sea.

The boy told him the names of several streets, pointing, and Daavid started off, following the boy's directions.

When Aryay and Yaakov awoke that morning they thought that Daavid had already gone to the washroom or to breakfast, but they did not see him in the washroom. Then Shlomo also awoke, and told them they were stupid, for it was plain that the new boy had run away, his things were gone. Instantly Yaakov searched under his pillow to make sure his fountain pen was safe. Then they inspected the room, but none of their things was missing.

Then Aryay said he had better go and tell Malka, but they stopped him, since surely it would come out that they had been fighting, and that was why the boy had run away. The monitor, Johanan, would tell how they had been fighting.

"What of it?" Yaakov demanded. "Nothing happened to him. He didn't have to run away."

"He did a good job," Shlomo admitted reluctantly. "I didn't even hear him, and I sleep as light as a watchdog."

"You sleep like a gassed cadaver with his mouth open," Yaakov flung at him.

They decided to have a look for the boy themselves first. Perhaps he was hiding in the stable or somewhere on the grounds. But Malka met them in the hallway and asked how it was with the new boy, and Aryay couldn't look into her eyes.

In Malka's office the story came out about the fight. But she was not angry. Instead she sent them out quickly to search the hill. She did not want to telephone Makor Gallil and alarm the boy's friends unless there was no other way.

They took a dozen other boys and hunted in pairs over the hills and fields. Aryay, since he was from an Arab country, spoke to the shepherds, asking whether they had seen the boy, and one, near the black tents, said he had seen a boy going to the road, and several of the children of the tent said they had also seen the boy.
. When they told this to Malka, she decided to telephone Makor Gallil, thinking that Daavid might have tried to make his way there. She placed the call. It would take a few hours.

The bus station was not so hard to find. It was a very big place, with entire streets of busses, and lines of people waiting. When his turn came at the booth Daavid said he wanted to go to the Dead Sea, offering the money the violinist had given him. The man gave him a ticket, and Daavid showed it to another man, who showed him which way to go. Everyone seemed a little amused at him, but no one asked too much.

Standing in line, waiting to get on the bus, a new feeling came upon Daavid. For now he was going somewhere himself, by his own doing, and in this way he felt that perhaps he was no different from all the other people who knew where and to whom they were going, for now he was no longer wandering, and he was no longer being carried like a stone in a handful of stones; he could tell the name—Yehuda Halevi, and the place—the Dead Sea. There he would at last enter his home.

He found a seat by the window. He did not want to ask anyone how far it was, or how long the journey would take, or how he would know the place when he came there, for surely he would know his father's house when he saw it.

The bus crossed a wide plain, then wound up a road with many twisting turns. Looking back, Daavid could see the whole distance even to the yellow sand and the sea. Then he looked forward, out the window, waiting to feel, at some moment, that this was the place.

But here again, after the cultivated flat land, the country was empty and the hills barren. Once or twice, among the hills of stones, he saw green places, where people might live. There were also hills in which ledges had been dug, like great wide steps, but the ledges were crumbling and dried and broken. Perhaps these were places such as Avram had spoken of, where people had lived long ago; vines and olive trees had grown on those ledges, and many people had moved along the paths on their donkeys. And now these places needed to be built anew. Daavid wondered if his father were building again on such a hill. He would work beside his father, carrying the fallen stones, and building.

The man next to him was reading some papers that he had taken out of a wrinkled portfolio. But once he looked up and said, "Where to, comrade?"

"I am going to the Dead Sea," Daavid replied.

"Aha." The man glanced at the pack that Daavid held on his lap. "On a hike all by yourself? Or have you a family there?"

"I have my family there."

"Aha. You know how to go? You will have to change at the station in Jerusalem."

"Yes," he said, for he did not want to seem lost. The bus wound upward, spinning around the hills, and then, on top of a high mountain, there was a very high statue, twenty times as tall as anyone. It was a woman holding a baby in her arms.

"Who is she?" Daavid asked of the man sitting with him.

"A mother and her child," the man said.

"Why is she there?"

"From there she looks out upon Jerusalem."

Daavid felt that it was a good sign for him, that she was there, with her baby in her arms. "Who put her there?" he asked.

"The Christians," his neighbor said, "for the whole world to see."

The bus had passed on, and Daavid turned to look back at the great mother. But perhaps after all her being there was not a sign for him. "Is she a Christian mother?" he asked.

The man smiled the same strange little smile that Daavid had seen on Avram and that seemed to be a Palestinian smile. "No, she was a Jewish mother," the man said.

Then they saw Jerusalem—a scattering of houses on a stony mountain. As the bus came to the first street, tanks were across the road, and soldiers made everybody get out of the bus and show their papers. This time they did not open his pack.

The bus went through a street and into a station. Daavid remembered that Jerusalem was to have been the city of his search, but now he knew where to find his family, and he did not care about Jerusalem. The man who had been sitting with him pointed to another bus and said, "There, comrade, there is your bus for the Dead Sea." It had not taken long to come, less than two hours, and in another hour they said he would be at the Dead Sea.

This time the bus was nearly empty, and it passed through another street and went out of the city. It went down, winding down an even more twisted road than the road coming up to Jerusalem, and the hills became yellow and then white, turning from fire to ashes. There was nothing on them, not even grass between the stones; they were like empty places in a dream, vast, distant, empty places through which one wound and wound, without ever reaching anywhere, and where nothing lived. The air became hot on his face, and he felt very tired. Looking out over the strange country, Daavid became afraid that nothing at all was true, that he was not really on his way to the place where his father lived, or where anyone could live. Everything had been a giant deception, a strange joke, such as older people played, just like the other senseless things they did. They tried to save everybody from sickness, and then they made war, and killed everybody; they said Eretz Yisroel was a homeland, and then they kept you out with warboats and tommy guns. And now surely it was their same joke; they said go there, go there! And you went, from Poland and from Germany and on boats and then running away, and finding the way, and at last you came there and it was their same joke, for it was a vast hole of emptiness, where nothing was, and nobody lived. It was a hole in the earth from long long ago.

The bus went deep into a cut between the mountains. The air was thick, and Daavid felt it pressing in his ears. But at last the bus issued from this narrow place into a region that was flat and gray, with deep cracks in the earth, like cracks in the burnt and dried clay on the inside of an oven. And everywhere there were small mounds, but the tops of the mounds were cut off flat, like heads cut off, and the sides were torn so that the layers of stone showed, with the flesh of earth torn away. It was indeed as though he had come to the very end of the world in his search, and if he could not find them here, they were nowhere on earth.

Camels ran across the burned earth; they were unharnessed, and naked, and looked like beasts from another time and another world.

And then, at the end of this plain, there was a sea, but it was darker than any other water. It was the Dead Sea.

Close to the sea there were wide square pens where the water lay very low, and in some of them there was no water, only white stuff, like the bleached dust of bones, on the bottom of the pens. And as the bus came to the sea, Daavid saw a factory with smokestacks and metal walls.

The bus stopped at a gate where a watchman was standing. Only a few men were on the bus, and they had passes to show the watchman, who then allowed them to go through the gate.

"Can I go inside?" Daavid asked the watchman. "I want to see Yehuda Halevi."

"You know not everyone can come in here," the watchman said. "You see what it says on the sign: *Entrance Forbidden*. In three languages. Is Yehuda a friend of yours?"

Daavid was tired, and tired of answering questions, and his voice was small. "I think maybe he is my father," he said wearily.

The watchman wrinkled his face like a wise old camel. "I know Yehuda Halevi," he said, "and I know his whole family, but I don't know you, so how can he be your father?"

"Then maybe he is my uncle," Daavid said desperately.

The watchman beamed, as one who is fond of people who make jokes. And the smile now was like all the smiles everywhere—everywhere they were kind to him, and yet they did not help him find what he sought.

"Maybe he is your brother—or even your sister!" the watchman said, pleased with his own humor. And then, even though he was not a British soldier, he wanted to see what was in Daavid's pack, saying, as if this too was a joke, "Maybe you want to blow up our plant." And at last, as Daavid said, "My name is Halevi too, Daavid Halevi," he took Daavid inside the gate.

The factory stood far from the gate. On a narrow railroad track were long trains of small open cars, filled with a white powder, like white earth. A giant scoop was lifting the white earth from flat-bottomed boats on the Dead Sea and loading the earth into the cars. As one of these trains rolled slowly past them, the watchman stepped onto the bumper at the end of the train and motioned to Daavid, who hopped on beside him, holding onto the rim of the last car. They rode toward the factory.

"This is potash," the watchman explained fondly. "And why do we labor, your father and your uncle and your brother and I? To take this stuff out of the sea and put it back into the earth!" This too seemed a great jest to him, and he followed his jest with a riddle. "Listen!" said the watchman to Daavid. "Here is a puzzle for you." He recited:

> "Brothers and sisters have I none,
> But this man's father
> Is my father's son.
> Who am I?"

The train went slowly, and the white flat fields of potash, drying in the sun, dazzled Daavid's eyes. The sun was hot, and the riddle was like a scarecrow, turning and turning slowly in the slow hot wind.— Who am I? Who am I?

They came to the factory. The air was filled with white dust, and inside, piles of the white potash were being carried on chainbelts high into the machinery, and great furnaces were revolving and churning, and there were clanking and hissing noises, and up in the swirling whiteness there were iron ladders and iron passageways among the giant curving pipelines and the huge vats, and up there in the whiteness Daavid saw two men—one of them an Arab with a kerchief and a black circlet on his head, the other bareheaded.

"Yehuda!" the watchman called, shouting above the noise of the machines. "Here is something for your dreams!"

The bareheaded man was the one who was called, for he leaned down toward them, trying to see through the mist, and he put his hand to his forehead as though he were indeed a dreamer, in the midst of the whirling machines.

He saw them and came down a few steps on the iron ladder, watching them as they approached through the tangle of tracks and conveyers.

"Careful," Yehuda called down to them. "Careful, my boy."

"Here is a lad," the watchman shouted, "who is your son and your nephew, and maybe he is your brother too!"

Yehuda came down the iron stairs until he was only a few steps above them. The Arab had also come down behind Yehuda to see what was happening.

Daavid went as close as he could, trying to see the man's face, but it was covered with white dust and sweat.

The watchman said ceremoniously, "Yehuda Halevi, here is Daavid Halevi."

The man passed his arm across his face to wipe away the grime, and his face came out clear and serious. He looked into Daavid's face and repeated his name, "Daavid Halevi?"

Daavid was afraid to let himself believe anything any more, for he had looked into the faces of so many men, and he had been ready to take any one of them, and yet not one of them had taken him. Still, though he no longer wanted to hope, his fullest hope was returning.

Even though the watchman had already said he knew Yehuda Halevi could not be his father, Daavid began to think, the watchman might have been joking all the time. Perhaps he had even been joking when he said he knew all of Yehuda's family, and that there was no missing son. For this was the end of the earth, the last place.

Daavid said, "I am looking everywhere for my family."

The man reached to a switchbox on the railing beside him and turned a handle on the machine. Slowly the machinery stopped. Then he came even closer to Daavid.

"The man in Tel Aviv told me you escaped from Poland," Daavid ventured.

"Yes." Yehuda Halevi looked at him carefully, and at his arm. "How old were you when everyone was taken away?"

"Five years old."

"And you remember everyone in the family?"

"Oh, yes!" Daavid said. "Did everyone escape? My mother too? And my brothers, with you and all my uncles? And—" He felt a little worried at the way the man was looking into his eyes now. As though they had something very hard to bear together.

"You remember them all?" the man said again.

Maybe he wanted to say that they had not all been able to jump from the train, and that the train had carried some of them away. Daavid could see them, as they were carried to the furnace, a great furnace, almost like the one in this place. And the white ashes.

But there was even more in the man's eyes. And Daavid saw what it was that this man could not say to him. It was over then, and finished. And this was the last place. He had to show that he was strong, so he said the thing himself.

"You're not my father," Daavid said.

Yehuda Halevi did not look away from his eyes. "No, Daavid. I'm not your father." He seemed to take a long, long breath. "I am your father's brother."

The words sounded and sounded, like a hammer that kept beating, now joyously, on the iron furnace behind them. He had almost given up believing, and now it was true! He had found his family!

The watchman was saying something strange. "Waking or dreaming, Yehuda?" he said, though he was smiling.

"You remember me? You recognize me?" Daavid inquired of his uncle.

"You've grown, Daavid!" Yehuda declared. "But you look just like your father!" He came down the last step and held both of Daavid's shoulders. "Good! Good that you found me! I'll take you home, and you'll stay with us! You remember your Aunt Chemda? And now we have a little baby, a cousin for you!"

"Yes, Uncle Yehuda, yes!" Daavid cried. All the men of the factory were thronging around them, and to them Daavid cried, "I've found my own uncle!"

They all touched him and felt him and put their hands on him, laughing, as though to make sure he was flesh and bone. They were strong men, with great bare muscles.

The watchman was explaining everything to them, as though it were a thing he alone had accomplished. "Halevi's nephew! I brought him to him! A real dream!"

And his uncle turned to the Arab behind him. "Look, Salich! My brother's son! He lived through everything!"

The Arab said, "If you want to take him home to your wife, I will watch the machine."

124

His uncle thanked the Arab. "Daavid, we'll go home to your aunt, right away!"

Walking by his uncle's side, Daavid started out of the factory. Now everything was good. Yet, one thing still remained. And if he asked it, all that he had found might lose its goodness.

"Uncle Yehuda," Daavid asked, "didn't you find my father here in Palestine?"

His uncle stopped, as though it was a matter that could not be spoken of fully and rightly while they were in movement. And then his uncle studied him, deciding what to say. "Not yet, Daavid," he said. "I haven't found him yet."

Daavid waited for his uncle to tell him more about his father, but Yehuda walked on a few steps and then stopped. "Look, Daavid," Yehuda said, calling his attention to a machine that was pouring white dust into sacks—it was the white powder after it had gone through the furnaces and the whirling and turning machines. "Look, Daavid, the potash from the bottom of the Dead Sea. We send it all over the world. It makes things grow."

"Did you look everywhere for my father?" Daavid persisted.

"Yes," his uncle said.

They began to walk again, passing the little hills of white potash alongside the walls of the factory. Uncle Yehuda told him how he had searched even in a place in Jerusalem, a big office where they had the names of all the families and all the people that had been found alive, the names gathered from all the camps and all the towns of Europe. He had asked them to search for the name of Halevi. When Daavid's father would be found, that office would have his name.

"In Jerusalem?" Daavid repeated.

"Yes," his uncle said. From there, he told Daavid, people were sent all over Europe and all over the world, to seek for the scattered families, and to send their names back to Jerusalem. Thus many families had been brought together—what remained of them.

Surely, Daavid felt, he had found the right way at last, for now his uncle, and all these men who were sent out over the world from Jerusalem, all would help him in his search.

They walked down the long road toward the Dead Sea, and

on both sides of them were the drying pens of water, flat and still under the sun. And walking easily beside his uncle, Daavid felt that he could at last ask a question that had troubled him, especially since that evening in the dining-hall of the settlement, when Avram and the others had asked him so many questions. It was a thing he could inquire only of his uncle, for an uncle would understand.

"Can I ask you something about my father, Uncle Yehuda?"

"Certainly, Daavid."

Daavid asked, "What was my father's name?" Again his uncle stopped and studied his face.

"But you know his name," Yehuda said.

"I can only remember 'papa,'" Daavid explained. "But that wouldn't be the name in the book in Jerusalem, would it?"

His uncle looked far out to the dark sea. "My brother's name was Yisroel," he said to Daavid. "That is how it would be written in the book."

Surely, yes surely, that was the name he had heard, far away and long ago. Yisroel. "Yes! That's his name!" Now he felt satisfied.

On the other side of the factory, along the shore of the Dead Sea, there was a place like an oasis, all green with palms and shrubbery; and as they neared it, Daavid saw that there were rosebushes, and sprayers whirled, watering the grass, and among the trees were cottages.

"This is where we live," Uncle Yehuda said.

It was a small white house, as Daavid had imagined it would be. And on the grass was a baby carriage, and near it lay a toy bear.

"Daavid," his uncle said, "I want to tell your aunt she has a big surprise coming. Wait here for a moment, yes?"

His uncle whistled a few notes toward the cottage. It was a family whistle, Daavid knew.

"Is that your signal whistle?" he asked.

"Yes." Yehuda smiled and whistled it again, just as he was going inside.

While Daavid waited, he practiced the family whistle softly to himself.

126

When Malka's call was put through to Makor Gallil only Hillel was in the secretariat. If Avram was near by, she asked, perhaps he could call him? But Avram, Hillel said, had gone over to the Arab village with some DDT and a sprayer to show them how to use the disinfectant.

Then Malka told Hillel what had happened.

No, Hillel had seen nothing of the boy. But even if Daavid were returning to Makor Gallil, he agreed it was unlikely that he could have reached the place so quickly. Probably he would yet appear. "A pity, a pity," Hillel kept saying, and promised to let her know immediately should the boy come home. Meanwhile he would discuss with the others how to start a search, and they would telephone her. It was nearly noon and he would see them in the dining-hall.

"Nothing is wrong, dear," Yehuda said quickly as he came into the house, for he knew that Chemda, like all wives, could not help a startled feeling of apprehension, seeing her husband coming home during working hours. She was in the kitchen and she had the baby settled in his playpen; she had been kneeling before the oven, and her face was flushed. Even in the midst of his excitement and worry about the boy outside, Yehuda did not fail to have the little feeling of surprise and pleasure that comes to a man on walking into his home unexpectedly and finding it all exactly as it is supposed to be while he is away.

Then rapidly Yehuda tried to make her understand what had happened. "It was simply impossible to disappoint him. You'll see. He had come all this way, and I was his last hope. And who knows? After all, we were a large family, we had relatives all over Poland, probably in Cracow too. He may be a little nephew, a few times removed."

It would not be his words, he knew. It would be what she decided in looking at his face. And, as always when he had done something impractical, he had to keep on talking, as though the words mattered, until Chemda saw in his face whatever it was that she wanted to know, perhaps only that his wish was pure. "So I had to tell him—you understand, dear—I am his father's brother."

127

The baby had become excited at seeing his father and was clamoring, making futile attempts to climb over his little fence, and Yehuda had to go to him for an instant.

"But this boy—he'll surely find out," Chemda said hesitantly.

"He's been through so much, he's confused, he'll believe us," Yehuda said rapidly as he lifted up the baby. "Listen, dear, I can't leave him waiting outside. You have only to remember, we lived in Cracow, my brother's name was Yisroel, and the boy is Daavid; remember that he had a big brother named Samuel, and his mother's name was Esther." He gave her the baby to hold.

"Esther," she repeated, touching back a loose strand of her hair. "But Yehuda, do you think you should do such a thing to the boy?"

It was all right. She was his Chemda. "It's already done," he said, smiling, and hurried to the door, whistling the family whistle for Daavid.

Instantly Daavid whistled back the tune. There was his uncle in the doorway. "She can't even imagine what's coming!" Yehuda said. And just then his aunt also came to the door. She was holding the baby.

His aunt was not like the big, round, important women that are aunts. She was young, with blond hair, and like pictures of beautiful ladies singing.

His uncle was smiling altogether happily over the surprise he was giving his wife. "Dear, do you know who this is?" he asked.

The aunt looked at Daavid, and looked at her husband, and looked more closely at Daavid, and then a sudden great joy came over her face. "Isn't it—could it be?" she asked. "Could it be little Daavid?"

"It's Daavid! Yisroel's son!" Yehuda said.

His aunt hugged him to her with her free arm, and the baby reached down from the other arm, laughing and touching his hair.

"Daavid!" his aunt cried. *"Shalom, shalom!* How wonderful that you found us! All by yourself!"

"By himself!" Yehuda said proudly, as though Daavid had done something that proved him worthy of the family. "Can you imagine! And how he got to Palestine! Wait till you hear!"

"Daavid, how do you like your cousin? His name is Akiba!" his aunt said, and then Daavid told her it was the same name as

128

that of the leader on their boat, and his uncle told him it was also the name of a great scholar and rabbi who had lived long ago, when the Jews were in Palestine, and who had fought with Bar Kochba against the Romans. Daavid said yes, he knew about the Romans.

Little Akiba took hold of his finger.

"You see, he's laughing, he likes you, he knows you are his cousin," Aunt Chemda said.

"He's only a year old," Uncle Yehuda told Daavid. "He can't talk yet."

"He can say mama and papa," Aunt Chemda said. "And now we will teach him to say Daavid."

His uncle began at once to teach the baby, repeating, "Daavid, Daavid. Akiba, say Daa-vid!"

They were inside the house, and it was a home, with candlesticks, and a picture of a grandfather on the wall, and curtains, and books on the table, and baby toys scattered on the floor. And there was another thing about the house, something that he knew from somewhere before. It was a sweet, warm odor that was all over the house.

He told his aunt, "Something smells nice, like I remember."

"It's Friday, Daavid," she said, "and I am baking the Sabbath bread."

"Like your mother did," Yehuda said.

His aunt pulled a loaf from the oven, and it was a braided kind of bread that he had once seen. Yehuda broke a piece from the loaf and gave it to him. "You know you shouldn't touch it before the Sabbath!" his aunt said, but she laughed as Yehuda answered, "When a little nephew finds us like this, it's the Sabbath already!"

"Be careful, it's hot," Chemda said to Daavid.

Yehuda took another piece, for himself. "Blow on it," he advised.

Daavid tasted the warm bread. It was good.

"A glass of milk right away," his aunt said, "and then I'll make you some lunch."

They had a place for him, in the room with his baby cousin Akiba, a place that would be his own. There, they said, he could put his little pack down and settle himself.

Chapter Seven

In the dining-hall Comrade Hillel found Zev and Nahama sitting with Miriam. Miriam took the news silently, almost as though she had expected it. She stopped eating and didn't look at anyone.

Nahama said Malka was probably right—the boy would try to come home to the people he knew, to the settlement.

"Do you think he can find his way here?" Zev asked.

"He's bright, and he knows how to take care of himself," Nahama said. "Besides, everyone would help him."

"He won't come here," Miriam said. "He will wander all over Palestine, looking for his family."

They looked at her, and they knew she was right.

The story spread through the room, and now Maccabee and Lazar and Yehudith came over, and a crowd formed around the table, arguing about what should be done. Maccabee wanted to go out at once and start searching for Daavid. "We should never have let him leave here," he said.

Zev tried to reassure them all. If the boy could make his way around Europe, no harm would come to him in Palestine.

"As long as he's among Jews," Lazar said. "But what if he—"

"Arabs don't eat children either," Zev said.

But they could not stand idly waiting, Maccabee insisted. He proposed to leave at once for the children's colony. But for that, Zev advised, he had better speak with Avram, since the newcomers were Avram's responsibility.

Good, the Giant said, he would set off immediately to find Avram in the Arab village. Miriam said she also would go. They would cross in the little boat.

"I'll have to go with you," Zev decided. "Yes, of course they are our friends, but it is always best if you can speak a few words of your friend's language."

Maccabee was impatient, but Zev, noticing that Miriam was wearing shorts, advised her to change and cover her legs. Among the Arabs, women did not go bare-legged.

They found Avram in the courtyard of the house of one of Jamal's cousins. Nassim was younger than Jamal, and wore a European jacket over his long white gown. He was speaking with Avram, and there was an amused, tolerant little smile on his lips. Maccabee would have interrupted them, but Zev drew the boy back, explaining that it would be disrespectful to show impatience in an Arab's house.

They waited, and the Arab spoke for a long time. Nassim was much esteemed in the village, Zev explained to Maccabee, for he had three wives. He had been very poor as a youth, and, like all the fellahin, he had cultivated the stony land of the hillside for an effendi to whom he remained always in debt. But when the Jews had come to buy land, Nassim had made a claim to several acres of the marshes, and with the money from the settlement of his claim, he had bought his wives, and with the labor of the wives he had imitated the ways of the settlers in digging canals and draining the swamp, and now he had good productive land and many children. Nassim had remained friendly to the settlement, and was even disposed to accept such new things as the DDT spray, since one of his wives was sick with the fever, and this Jewish trick might work, as had other Jewish magic. It would be useless to try to explain to him that malaria came from mosquitoes. But unless the Arab villages in the neighborhood were also cleansed of the carrier, the settlement was not safe from malaria.

There was a gathering in the courtyard, watching Avram's demonstration. He had the spray tank strapped to his back and was treating an open shed where goats, chickens, and other household animals were bedded. In a dark extension of the shed an old woman of the household was mashing grain on a stone.

Jamal now testified, as his cousins and townsmen watched the spray. "In my house," he said, "the flies fell from the wall, like rain."

"It will not heal those who are already sick," Avram told them, "but it will keep the sickness from coming to those who are well."

An Arab youth wanted to try the instrument, and Avram gave him the spray rod to hold and then transferred the carrying tank to his back. At last Avram came over to them, and Zev explained what had happened.

There was no need to be alarmed, Avram said. The boy would find his way. No one would hurt him.

"He might hurt himself," Miriam said. She knew that her remark sounded dramatic to Zev. But at least Avram had known how it was, that night when she had found Daavid by the river.

The best thing to do, Avram said, would be to telephone Jerusalem to put out word for the settlements to be on the look-out for Daavid. And if nothing was heard by morning, they would go themselves to the children's village, and from there start a search for him.

Daavid wet his hair, and smoothed it down, and put on the clean shirt from his pack; then he went back into the other room. His aunt had put on a white dress, which was pressed smooth, and he had seen his uncle shaving, and now Yehuda, too, wore a fresh white shirt, and the baby, also freshly dressed, was sitting in his highchair and was being so good, Aunt Chemda said, that he must know it was the Sabbath.

The table was covered with a white cloth. Daavid saw his aunt take the bread that smelled so good, put it on the table, and cover it with a silk cloth, with pictures and writing on it. She then placed candles in the two silver candlesticks that stood on the shelf, among the books. "Do you want to put them on the table for me?" she asked. He took one in each hand; they were heavy. He set them carefully on the table.

"They are from the other country," Yehuda said. "We brought them with us. They belonged to my mother and father—your grandparents."

"Do you see any matches there, Daavid?" his aunt asked.

He found the matches near the ash tray and brought them to her. "Why are you lighting the candles?" he asked, for there was electricity in the house.

"Because it is the eve of the Sabbath, the holy day of rest," his uncle said. "You know about the Sabbath, Daavid?"

"Yes," he said, but uncertainly. Miriam had told him some things, he said; she had said that the Sabbath was a religion.

"Miriam was the lady that came with me on the boat," he explained to them.

Yes, his uncle said, the Sabbath was part of the religion of the Jews. "We in this house are not very religious, Daavid," he said. "You see I am smoking, and if I were very religious, I would stop smoking when the Sabbath comes, because that is forbidden. And we are supposed to wear our hats," he said, "like my father did. For in those days people believed more in the outward signs of religion, such as covering their heads before God."

"But the candles are a sign of religion too," Daavid said.

"Yes. Some of the signs we keep," his uncle said. "The important ones."

Then his aunt picked up Yehuda's hat and gave it to him with an odd little smile, and he put it on, with the same odd little smile, and she gave Daavid his beret, and he put it on too.

Then she lit the candles and bent her face toward them. She moved her hands over the flames, and then touched her forehead with her hands, while she whispered some words over the candles.

"What is my aunt saying?" Daavid asked.

"She is thanking God for having saved us and brought us together."

Daavid watched the movement of her hands over the little points of fire. "I think my mother did that at home," Daavid said. He was trying to remember.

"Of course she did," his uncle said.

His aunt finished her prayer and lifted up her face. Her eyes were beautiful.

"Now the Sabbath is come," his uncle said. And it was so, as though someone good had come into the house.

They put the baby to bed, and Daavid sat with him until he was surely sleeping, while his aunt was in the other room, placing the food on the table. Through the open door he could see her.

"Is he asleep?" she whispered.

He looked again at his baby cousin, who was sleeping so pleasantly; his face was round, and his limbs were chubby and unblemished, and it was so good, the way people thought of

133

their babies, every breath and every second, caring for them and watching over them.

"He is asleep," Daavid said, and moved noiselessly toward the other room. They were just sitting down at the table. When Daavid had taken his place, his uncle spoke some holy words, and then uncovered the Sabbath bread, and broke a small piece for each of them. And he poured them each a glass of wine.

The wine was something Daavid had never tasted. He touched the glass to his lips and tilted it until the liquid slipped into his mouth, and in his heart Daavid felt that it was right that he should taste a new thing, as he was tasting happiness.

"Do you remember, Daavid," his uncle said, "how the family sang songs at the table every Sabbath eve?" And his uncle began to sing, and Aunt Chemda sang with him.

It was a song of the Sabbath. "She cometh as a bride," they sang. "Oh, welcome to the Sabbath bride, the bride who cometh from Heaven, the Bride in whom there is peace."

They sang, and the melody seemed to come back of itself to Daavid's throat, and then the words came to his lips, finding their way, as people do who enter a room they have known long ago.

He was singing too.

On Sabbath day, in the morning, the whole family went along the shore to a beach. They took Akiba in his carriage, and part of the way Daavid pushed the carriage on the firm sand near the water's edge. He was walking barefoot.

There were several apartment houses built in a circle near by, where other families lived, and there was a café with radio music, and there were beach umbrellas, and under one of these they settled themselves. Yehuda and Chemda wanted Daavid to try the water first, to feel the wonder of floating on it, for this sea was of a special kind of water that kept people afloat. But they told him to be careful to keep it out of his nose and eyes, for it was filled with salt and would sting.

He floated on the water. It was indeed as they had said, a strange sea, for the water did not suck people down to drown them, it held them aloft, and Daavid wondered why it was called the Dead Sea, for instead it was a sea where you could not die. The water was warm. He swam a little, and got water into his nose; the salt stung, and when he came out of the sea Yehuda and Chemda laughed at him. But soon the stinging passed.

Then his aunt and uncle went into the water, and Daavid sat under the umbrella, minding his little cousin. He had brought his flute, and now he began to play the tune he had learned when riding on the donkey with Mustafa. Then he tried to pick out the tune of the family signal. He leaned over and played it to Akiba. The baby stared and reached out to him, grasping the flute firmly in his hand.

"Say Daavid," Daavid repeated. "Akiba, say Daa-vid!"

His baby cousin waved the flute, laughing. The sun was warm. From out on the water where Daavid could see them, his aunt and uncle waved to him. They were lying on the water, talking.

The couple were far enough out so that Daavid could not hear them.

Again it was the question of the boy. As for his upkeep, Yehuda said, it really would not be a great problem. One more person did not make a great difference in the family.

No, Chemda said. They had not placed a one-child limit on the family. And though this one was rather quickly grown, still—
"But there is one thing we must do," she said.

Then Yehuda knew she would make him face the real question. "You are going to say we have to tell him."

"You know it yourself," Chemda said.

They lay very still on the water, as on a bed. Yehuda stared into the cloudless sky and found no answer.

"But we can't tell him," he said.

"The truth is bound to come out one way or another," Chemda insisted. "It's better to tell him now, ourselves. We will tell him that it's the same to us, that we want him to stay with us anyway."

Nothing moved in the sky. "If we tell him now," Yehuda said, "he will simply go away."

The gate watchman, Smulik, came along the beach. He too was dressed for the Sabbath—his shirt was white, his trousers were pressed. And with him were a boy and a girl. The boy was

135

larger than Daavid, with freckled arms, and the girl, who was Daavid's size, wore glasses, and she was walking carefully in her Sabbath clothes.

"*Shabbat shalom,* Daavid!" Smulik said.

Daavid thought of a joke. "Can you say Sunday *shalom* and Monday *shalom* too, and all the week like that?" he asked. He felt light and good.

But Smulik's boy answered him very seriously. "On weekdays we merely say *shalom,* peace," he declared, "but on the Sabbath we say *Shabbat shalom* because it is the traditional Sabbath greeting of peace and rest." His face was long as an egg, just like his father's.

The gatekeeper listened to his son with wrapt approval. Then he introduced the children to Daavid. Their names were Reuven and Lami. The little girl had taken the toy bear from the baby carriage and was arranging its ruffled clothing. "These are my children," Smulik said, but at the same moment Lami put the toy in his hands and he fondled it and she laughed at him, and he declared, "Sometimes they make me wonder who is the child, I or they? You know, Daavid," Smulik philosophized, "in this world we can't be sure of anything."

The boy, Reuven, was taking things out of his pocket—glass tubes, the size of a finger. He tied a string around the neck of one of the tubes, and now he bent by the water's edge, and cast the tube into the water, and drew it back with the string, thus scooping it full of water. He held the filled tube up to the light, squinting through it, and then he took out a cork, stoppered the tube, put it back in his pocket, and began to fill another tube.

"That's right," Reuven agreed with his philosophical father. "In this world you can't even be sure of nature. Some water, things sink in it, and this water, things float in it."

Lami was staring at Daavid. "And some people have sense," she declared, "and some people put tubes full of water in their pockets and sit on them and break them."

Lami wanted to be friends with him, Daavid thought, but if he were friendly to her, then perhaps her brother would be driven away. With her brother, he could come every day to the water and find out things. What would float in the sea, besides people? Would rocks float in it? And the boy was doing something else now. He held a thermometer, like doctors sometimes used, in the water.

Reuven announced the temperature and took out a little book and wrote it down.

"It's good and warm here, eh, Daavid?" Smulik said, settling lazily on the sand. "Better than living by the icy Baltic."

The icy Baltic? Daavid wondered was there another sea in Palestine that had ice in it?

"The Baltic is on the other side of Europe," Reuven informed him.

But surely, Smulik said, Daavid remembered when he lived in the same city as his Uncle Yehuda, in a port by a cold icy sea, the port of Gdynia? That sea was the Baltic.

"He was too little to remember the name," Lami said. "We lived in Tel Aviv when I was a baby but I never knew it was on the Mediterranean Sea."

But Daavid remembered very well that there had been no sea where he had lived. "We lived in Cracow," he said.

Smulik started to talk very fast. Yes, of course, Cracow, that was later, when the family moved from Gdynia, and he talked rapidly about the Dead Sea. It was the richest and strangest sea in the world, he said, filled with all sorts of valuable minerals. It was also called the salt sea, and in olden days it had been known as the asphalt sea.

"It was in the days of Josephus that it was known as the asphalt sea," Reuven declared.

"My children know everything! They know more than their father. You too will know everything," Smulik promised Daavid. "Ah, you children will be able to build a whole new life out of this dead sea! Imagine, in the factory they do all kinds of research. Reuven is going to be a chemist and do research too. In this sea are millions of tons of magnesium. And do you know what can be made out of magnesium? Airplanes, collapsible houses, flying automobiles!"

"There are nine hundred and eighty million tons of magnesium deposited here," Reuven said, and he spoke directly to Daavid. "We even have a plan to make electricity out of this sea!"

Could electricity be made out of water? Daavid asked. And Reuven explained that it had to do with the height of the mountains around them, because the Dead Sea was like a well lying deep in the earth. If water were brought by a giant pipe from the real sea, the sea near Tel Aviv, then that water would have to fall all the way from the top of those mountains into the Dead Sea, and in falling it would turn wheels, and the wheels would make electricity.

"The water has to fall twelve hundred feet to get down here, Daavid," Reuven declared. "According to my plan, that will make two hundred and twenty thousand kilowatts of electricity per hour."

Daavid had wanted to ask if that other sea, the Baltic, was far from Cracow, but now the question went from his mind, for Reuven was telling him how great factories could be operated with all that electricity. They would take many substances out of the Dead Sea, like he had in his test tubes, and they would produce all kinds of new inventions in those factories.

"That's nothing!" Lami said. "That's just an old plan from America. I have a real Palestinian plan, that will make three times as much electricity, and everybody will have electric cars and boats and stoves and refrigerators. And the whole country will be irrigated!" she declared. "All the bare hills will be gardens!"

Daavid looked at the chalky bare mountains around them, and he could almost see them bursting forth with banana trees and vines and yellows and reds and purples.

But Reuven did not believe his sister and demanded to know how her plan would work.

"It's still a secret from you," she said.

Then Daavid suddenly felt a grandness, as though he and his friends could take the whole sea and all the mountains in their hands. "I have a plan, too!" he said. "My father is a big engineer, and he will come and empty out the water so that we can dig up all the minerals, and then we will fill it up again from the ocean, and make electricity, and empty it out, and fill it up!"

Reuven was staring at him uncertainly, just as he had stared at his sister.

"Daavid," said Smulik the watchman, patting his head, "if you have a plan for the Dead Sea, you are already a Palestinian!"

Then Yehuda and Chemda came out of the water. Daavid

meant to ask his uncle about when they had moved to Cracow, but just then the baby Akiba stood up excitedly and waved his arms. Lami said the baby was really dancing to see his mother and father, and everybody laughed because the baby was so happy.

Smulik was talking and talking. "The most wonderful time in life is to be a baby!" he said, bending down and making faces and trying to talk like a baby to Akiba. "Look how happy he is! He knows his father and mother will take care of him! He has no problems! No problems!" The watchman made his funny camel-faces again, and Lami laughed at her father.

"Some people are babies all their lives!" she said.

Chemda told Daavid he was an excellent baby watcher; and now she said it was his turn to amuse himself.

"Akiba knows the family tune!" Daavid said. "Listen!" And he played the little tune on his flute. But just this time his baby cousin paid no attention. Akiba wanted only his mother, and she picked him up, swinging him high, and he was laughing.

Lami wanted Daavid to go for a walk with her. She said she would show him where Lot's wife had been changed into a pillar of salt.

Reuven told his sister, "That's because she was a woman who talked too much. And anyway it is only a legend."

Daavid walked slowly with Lami, until he was sure that Reuven was following only a little way behind them.

The grown people watched the children walking, in the ease of the Sabbath, and were satisfied that all was going well for Daavid. Then Smulik turned on Yehuda, as one righteously offended. "Yes, it may be well for the boy," he said, "provided nothing happens to break his illusion."

Yehuda looked at him, unable to hide a little guilt and shame. "What do you mean? What illusion? You and your philosophy!"

Smulik confronted him sternly. "Yehuda, it is bad enough to deceive a child," he said, "but why do you have to deceive a friend? Just now I nearly said something that would have plunged him back into the ice of reality. Yehuda, Gdynia and Cracow are not the same place."

Yehuda sighed. "Smulik, I—I couldn't disappoint him, so I—I invented it all on the spur of the moment."

Chemda put the baby back into his carriage and gave him his toy bear.

Smulik shook his head sorrowfully over his friend's impulsiveness. "It will not help, Yehuda," he said. "The boy will find out."

"Yes. And then it will be even worse for him," Chemda said.

"Why do you do things so emotionally?" Smulik persisted. "Consider. Maybe he does have a family somewhere, and in that case you are really preventing him from finding them. Maybe he has people who are attached to him, and you are hurting them, too."

"Convince him, Smulik!" Chemda pleaded.

"But what can I do now," Yehuda begged, "so as not to hurt the child?"

"Without hurting," Smulik declared, "nothing is real. There was a French philosopher, Descartes," he recited, and Yehuda saw how easy it was for Smulik to escape from any problem. "And this philosopher said, 'I think, therefore I am.' Now how would a Jew say it? A Jew would say, 'I suffer!'"

"You are still a Russian, Smulik," Chemda declared.

In the settlement, breakfast on the Sabbath was an hour later than on weekdays, but Miriam was awake at the weekday hour. On the way to the dining-hall she passed the secretariat; the door was locked. All night there had been no word; or if some news had come, they had not told her.

In front of the cottage where the Feldheims lived she saw Zev and Weisbrod. They were kneeling in the little garden by the porch, where there were several rosebushes. Weisbrod was planting something there, under the Palestinian's guidance.

"Shabbat shalom," Zev said.

Miriam asked if there had been any news. Zev shook his head, and his usual equanimity seemed even to be deepened by the Sabbath calm. Weisbrod went on patting the earth with his thin, skeletal hands. His silence while Daavid was being discussed somehow reminded her of the way it had been in the camps when people disappeared.

"Can't we telephone the children's colony?" Miriam asked.

140

"Perhaps later," Zev said.

In the dining-hall the tables were still empty. Miriam sat down not far from the door. One of the girls, the dark and pretty little Yemenite, appeared from the kitchen and asked if she had a Sabbath work-turn and wanted her breakfast early? No, she would wait.

Maccabee came in with Dvora and Lazar. They took places at another table. But young Dvora leaned toward her, saying, "We saw Hillel. There's no news. We must make Avram do something."

Especially from Maccabee, Miriam felt a silent accusation, for it was she who had insisted on sending Daavid away. But all night long she had gone over the problem. The fact that the boy had run away again was even further proof that she had been right, that he needed a special kind of adjustment. It was no sign that he should have remained at Makor Gallil, but proved only that his trouble must be even more urgent than they had known. And yet if something had happened to him, how could she ever keep from blaming herself?

The servers came along with their trays. There was white bread for the Sabbath. People came and sat at the same table with her. For one thing Miriam was grateful—among the numbers at the commune it was possible to lose oneself, to be alone. She did not try to recognize their faces. And today in any case they looked like different people in their Sabbath clothes; they looked a little like visitors to the settlement.

Many of them brought their children into the dining-hall on this day, and through the long horizontal window Miriam saw others parading on the veranda or frolicking on the grass with their children, tossing them into the air or rolling in mock wrestling matches with them.

Those who had been at her table finished and left, and the servers came to clean the table. Someone said, "Is something wrong, Miriam?" And she looked up and noticed it was Ziona who was wiping the table. The girl already had a Sabbath work-turn.

"No, nothing," Miriam said and smiled.

"Don't worry about Daavid," Ziona said. "He's an old partisan. He'll find his way home. It will be good to have him with us

141

again." Ziona meant no accusation, Miriam knew; Ziona was not malicious.

Then Avram entered. He was wearing his everyday clothes. He came directly toward her, picking a plate of food from a passing food cart on his way. As he sat down, the young people came from their table and gathered around him.

"We haven't heard anything," Avram said.

"Isn't there anything we can do to find him?"

"Couldn't we put a notice in the paper?" Tirza asked. "Then if anyone sees Daavid, they will send him home."

"It's the Sabbath," Avram pointed out. "The newspaper offices are closed; but if Daavid is not heard of by night, I'll telephone to the *Davar,* in Tel Aviv."

"And what of the police?" Miriam asked. "At least they could be notified."

"The police!" Ziona said scornfully, as though from long experience. "What good are the Palestine police? They're too busy searching for Irgunists to kill, to bother about a little lost boy. Especially a Jew."

The circle around the table grew larger. "There's only one thing to do," Maccabee said. "And that's to go out and search all Palestine for Daavid."

"But on the Sabbath," Blaustein pointed out, "there is no way to go. The busses don't run."

"There are the Arab busses," Amos mentioned.

"Would you go on an Arab bus?" Ziona asked.

"Why not?" Avram said. There could be no harm in taking a trip to the children's village to find out exactly what had happened.

They decided that Miriam should go with Avram.

On the way they spoke little. She was crowded on a small seat against a black-robed Arab woman who held a child in her lap; baskets and sacks filled the leg space. Avram stood for a good part of the way, and finally found a seat on the other side of the bus. Occasionally he looked back toward her, almost idly. She could not understand how he managed to remain so relaxed. He was not unconcerned for the boy. But now he seemed to be carrying on a conversation in Arabic, exchanging cigarettes with his neighbors.

At moments she felt there was a hostility in the bus. At various stops along the road other Sabbath travelers got on, until the bus load was a third Jewish. Though one or two, like Avram, seemed to know Arabic and to make deliberate attempts at friendliness, most of the settlers, brawny and bare-armed and filled with holiday exuberance, created a separateness in the bus. A few of the Arabs could be seen casting hateful glances; they would not shift their sacks and baskets that cluttered the aisle to make room for the Jews. At another stop, where a little group of Jews were waiting, the bus went by without halting, and the driver looked at the fare-collector, and they exchanged peculiar smiles. She thought of the child wandering alone in this country.

Miriam was blaming herself, Avram knew. For this reason he had brought her along to see Malka Orloff. Actually there was nothing Miriam could do, but this attempt at activity would help her.

As the Arab bus passed only on the main road, they had to walk up the last mile to the colony. Her own child would have been how old by now? Five or six. A baby, she had said. Certainly not as old as Daavid. After a while he might again suggest that she work with children. Perhaps in a children's village like this. That might be a good plan both for Daavid and Miriam. He was sure the boy would turn up.

Several children met them at the gate. Whom were they coming to visit? the youngsters demanded. Were they somebody's uncle and aunt? Somebody's big sister and brother?

They weren't coming to visit anybody, Avram confessed. They were coming for someone who wasn't there. What about Daavid? Had he turned up?

Aryay was among the boys. "No," the dark-skinned boy said, "Daavid went back to his *kibbutz*."

"He had a fight," a smaller boy offered.

And walking into the grounds with them, the children related the story.

"I was right," Yaakov repeated indignantly. "He hasn't got a family! It was just a picture he drew himself. You're not his family, are you?"

"No," Miriam said. "You were right."

Malka Orloff gave them tea in her office. It was a pity, she said, that the incident had taken place on the first night, for it had seemed to her that the boy was making a good start with his comrades and might get along very well.

"He must have felt deserted and alone," Miriam said. "That was why he got into the fight."

As Avram had expected, Malka saw at once what was troubling the girl. "No," she said, "you did right to bring him here. Every one of these children has struggled with the same problem. It's only that in some of them it is worse than in others."

Miriam responded. "Yes, in Daavid the problem is acute." She was easier with Malka, Avram saw. She had at last found someone who spoke in her own terms.

"In difficult cases," Malka said, "we sometimes consult Dr. Mayer of Jerusalem."

"Professor Alfred Mayer?" Miriam asked. A note of awakening was in her voice.

"Yes," Malka said, smiling a little. He had escaped from Vienna, and he was in Jerusalem.

"You know him?" Avram asked Miriam.

And instantly he felt her withdrawing again. "I know of him," she said.

But he saw that when the boy was found, she would want to try the way of the difficult cases, and already there was a resistance in Avram to admitting that the boy might have to go through anything that was for the unhealthy. Avram knew that he would have to curb his resistance, that he was wrong, that there were things that did not exist in the open air, and that of these dark inner things these minds knew better than he; and yet he would want it to be, for Daavid, as for any child, that health came from the air, from the fields, from comrades.

On the other side of the potash factory there was a settlement, and there was something special to see at this place, Reuven promised. It was more important than historic legends of women turned into pillars of salt—though history was important too. In this settlement, he promised, Daavid would see how the salt was soaked out of the soil.

Was that how salt for eating was secured? Daavid asked.

No, Reuven explained, it was a different matter entirely. It was a matter of poisons in the earth. There were many kinds of poisonous salts that killed living things. They killed everything that grew, and therefore this was the region of death, the Dead Sea.

And before them, like an oasis, was the settlement, with its rows of white houses, and lanes of tall trees, and fields of corn. How did these things grow, Daavid asked, after what Reuven had said?

This was just the proof of what he said, Reuven declared. They came to muddy fields, and then there were ponds of water fenced by lanes of mud. That was how it was done, Reuven explained. Each pond was filled with clean water from the Jordan, and as the water soaked down through the earth it carried down the poisonous salts, and then things could be planted in the purified soil, and they grew. "The biggest tomatoes in Palestine grow here!" he declared triumphantly. They were certainly bigger, he said, than the tomatoes at Makor Gallil!

Lami took off her shoes. "It feels wonderful," she said. "It's soft between your toes."

Daavid hesitated, but Reuven began to take his shoes off too. He said he wanted to collect some specimens of the soil from under the water. They formed in a line and waded to the middle of the pond.

All this was a triumph of chemistry, Reuven said. He was going to be a chemist. "In Father Avraham's time," he declared, "the Dead Sea was all the way up to here. And when it dried out, it left all kinds of chemicals." And then he confided that he had even a better plan than soaking the soil to make things grow; he would find the chemicals in the soil that made the tomatoes grow so big. "Do you know that you can grow everything only with chemicals?" he demanded of Daavid. "Just chemicals and water. You don't even need land. We could take all these chemicals out of the Dead Sea, and we could grow enough to feed all the Jews, and bring them all to Palestine from the camps, and make a chemical factory for food for everybody, and everybody could live in skyscrapers like in America, and we could even have enough food to send to all the starving Chinese. We don't even need to slave on the soil. Let the Arabs keep all the soil, and slave for the effendis, plowing with their camels and donkeys!"

Lami was scooping up mud from the bottom and building an island in the pond. The edge of her dress was wet. "You don't know what you're talking about!" she accused her brother. "Don't listen to him, Daavid. It's against our ideal, what he says. Our ideal is to reclaim this land!"

Reuven was silent, as though she had really caught him saying something wrong.

"How do you reclaim the land?" Daavid asked.

"You take dead land and make it come to life!" Lami said.

Daavid reached down and took a handful of the mud. It was cool, and felt firm. "Can you make dead things come to life?" he asked, looking at Reuven.

"Certainly!" Reuven said. "The French made a whole new coast of fertile land out of sand, and in America the desert of Nevada has been irrigated and reclaimed. And even here, all this land is being born again."

"Can people be born again?" Daavid asked.

Now they were all three building the island. Reuven began to form a fortress in the center of it. He held the mud in his hands, and pondered, just like his father, the watchman. "Rebirth," he said, "that is still an unsolved question. Some people believe it can happen. This is the theory of metempsychosis."

"Of what?" Daavid asked.

And Reuven repeated his word, "Metempsychosis."

Lami said to Daavid, "If you could be born again, would you choose the same mother and father?"

He couldn't even answer. His throat closed.

But Reuven spoke readily. Of course he loved his father, he said, but if emotions were not to be considered, he would choose a great scientist, like Einstein, or Eddington, or Weizman for his father.

Lami said, "I would choose the same mother and father, only instead of you for a brother, I would choose Daavid." She made two people and put them on the roof of the castle.

In his fingers Daavid felt the reborn earth taken from under the water. Earth was what people were made of. Long ago, someone, perhaps his father, had told him this.

Hassan Effendi of the Government Department of Antiquities still permitted himself to go to Tel Aviv occasionally. It saddened him that it was becoming more and more inadvisable to be seen there. He had received broad hints from more than one of his relatives. The air of Tel Aviv was not healthy for an Arab, they said. And he found little clippings on his desk about the return of the Mufti from Germany. Nevertheless, he was sure he would get a more certain sign, before he absolutely had to stop. It would be a pity to be able to go there no longer, since he was fond of the European cafés, the movement of the crowds, the accelerated tempo. He even considered whether it would be better to leave Palestine until the ugliness was over. To go someplace where a man could look at pictures and enter a concert hall without glancing behind him.

On this Saturday morning a cousin came and plagued him for an hour for a contribution to the "scout fund," even hinting that it was not safe to refuse. Earnestly his cousin explained that the Husseinis were coming back, in full power, and there was no use trying to resist them—one had to live. In the end Hassan made the contribution, pretending, in a feeble joke, that he hoped it would be used for musical instruments. His cousin laughed raucously and culminated the joke by imitating the music of a tommy gun.

As revenge, in the afternoon Hassan openly drove in his own car from Jaffa to Tel Aviv. On Saturday afternoons, at the Café Ginati, there was a good band, and there would be crowds, and among them probably many of his Jewish acquaintances.

And so it happened that he recognized, at once, Dr. Nahum Shahar, with whom he had often discussed Arabic poetry. Dr. Shahar was with his wife and another couple. Hassan sat at their table. They were decent and carefully avoided political subjects. Of course he still went to the concerts, Hassan said. They had not seen him in Tel Aviv because recently he had been driving up to Jerusalem for the symphony. And in passing he told the anecdote of the little son of the violinist Halevi, who had been in a fight and had run away from school.

But the Shahars were acquainted with Halevi and said that the man was unmarried! And when Halevi himself appeared at the Ginati, the story was told to him.

The musician became rather serious. He had been uneasy about the boy ever since the rehearsal. "Where did you pick him up?" he asked Hassan.

They concluded that the boy must have come from the children's village. And perhaps it would be worth while to telephone Malka Orloff, since the child was wandering around in such a strange way.

When Malka Orloff received the call, Avram and Miriam had already gone back to their settlement, having decided to carry on the search through the newspapers. She relayed the news to the settlement at once. There was no longer any need to be worried. The boy would surely be found at the Dead Sea, where he had gone to look for a worker named Halevi. They could reach the factory first thing in the morning.

Chapter Eight

Uncle Yehuda was not at the table for breakfast. He had gone out on a little errand, Aunt Chemda said. Daavid decided to wait for breakfast until his uncle returned. Aunt Chemda had made a glass of juice for him, squeezed out of oranges, and she said he could at least drink that, while waiting. It tasted good. Now she was slicing more oranges in two, to make orange juice for Akiba. She said it would give the baby straight legs.

"Let me do it," Daavid said.

While he was squeezing the oranges, his aunt told him he was going to go to school. After Yehuda went to work, she would take him there.

"The same school as Reuven and Lami?" Daavid asked.

"Yes," his aunt said.

He was a little worried, and his aunt saw this. "Aren't you glad to go to school with your friends?" she asked.

"They know so much," Daavid said. "Even Lami."

His aunt laughed. "They don't know more than you. You know other things. You tell them what you know, and they'll tell you what they know. They'll help you catch up in school."

Someone came to the kitchen door just then, but it was not his uncle. It was Smulik, the watchman. His face was dark. He asked for Yehuda, and when Chemda said that Yehuda had gone out for a few minutes, Smulik stood there, without even talking.

"Is something wrong?" Chemda asked.

"No, no. Who knows what is right and what is wrong?" he said, but it was not said like one of his jokes.

"I'm going to school," Daavid told Smulik. "With Reuven and Lami."

"Oh?" That was all the watchman had to say.

Then Daavid heard the family whistle. He ran to open the door. Yehuda gave Daavid the package he was carrying. "It's for you!" he said. "Salich went to Jerusalem yesterday, and I asked him to buy a few things."

Daavid looked to his aunt. In one way he wanted to keep the whole package as it was, to keep the feeling of receiving it into his hands. And if he had to open it, then he wanted that moment to be only before the family.

"Open it," she said.

Yehuda noticed Smulik and said, "*Shalom*," and as he saw the watchman's face, he added jokingly, "You've had a nightmare?"

"I wish it were a nightmare," Smulik said. "Listen. I have to talk to you. I've been at the plant already."

Smulik did not want him there, Daavid felt. It was a thing for grown people.

"Don't you want to open your package in your room, Daavid?" Aunt Chemda said. "It's a surprise just for you!"

He took the package to his room.

The moment Daavid was gone, Smulik said, "Listen, they've telephoned already about him."

"Who?" Yehuda asked.

"Avram, from Makor Gallil. He is a runaway," Smulik explained. "He ran away from there, and then they took him to the children's village, and he ran away again."

"He won't run away from us," Yehuda said. "He is happy here."

"Avram is coming here," Smulik said.

"But they don't have to take him away!" Chemda said. "We'll tell Avram we want to keep the boy. He has nobody closer than us, in their settlement."

"We'll tell him I'm his uncle," Yehuda said. "And that's all."

Chemda smiled patiently. "You can't pretend to them," she said.

"But if they know the truth," Yehuda worried, "they might not agree. They might have their own ideas for the boy."

"You have to consider the boy," Smulik said. "The boy has a real problem."

"Wait, let me think," Yehuda said. He was beginning to feel pressed, harassed.

"Your thinking is emotional," Smulik declared. "Be logical. You cannot solve his problem with an illusion."

"Smulik, leave me be!" Yehuda cried. It was not a moment for fine-spun analysis. He knew he was getting excited. Why had he started the whole deception? Whatever he did now would hurt the child.

Smulik gazed at him with his most irritating look of philosophic calm. And Daavid was already coming into the room, grinning shyly, holding his new clothes on his arm. "I love you like a brother," Yehuda said, "but this is my problem."

"You see, you emotionalize everything!" Smulik declared. "You never even had a brother. Logically—"

Daavid heard Smulik's words. At first he wasn't sure that they had a meaning for him. He didn't understand why Smulik stopped himself. And the look on Smulik's face was the same as before, on the beach, when he had mentioned the icy Baltic. The last words echoed, "You never even had a brother," and then the whole thing was clear in Daavid's mind. If Yehuda had never had a brother, then he couldn't be an uncle. And then it was true that he had lived by the Baltic Sea, and not in Cracow.

Daavid stood still. The three people also stood motionless. He could not look into their eyes.

Then Chemda came over to him. She put her hands on his shoulders. "Daavid, we want you to live with us," she said. "We want you to be our son, and Akiba's big brother."

Yehuda said, "Daavid, I told you I was your uncle because we want you so much. We want you to stay with us, Daavid. We are like one big family anyway, our people, all that is left of us."

Nothing reached him, of what they were saying. He knew only that if Yehuda was not his uncle, he was in the wrong place. "My father would never come to your house to find me," he said. "You are not my father's brother."

"We'll find your father, Daavid," Yehuda promised. "I will go to Jerusalem myself, and search there, in the office, where they have all the names."

The new clothes were still hanging on his arms, the jacket and the trousers and the shirt. Daavid held them out to Chemda, but she would not take them back. "Your friend Avram is coming," she said. "When he comes, we'll tell him we want you to stay with us. Won't you stay, Daavid?"

Now he felt that all of them, Avram and all the rest of them, were trying to trap him and hold him, in one place or another, like in the camps. They didn't want him to search. He could not speak to anyone. He went to his room.

It was time for the men to go to work. Smulik kept looking at his wristwatch. Yehuda waited until the last moment, but what more could he say to the boy?

Chemda thought they had best let him alone, let him get over the shock. After Avram came, they could all talk to the boy together.

Again Smulik looked at his watch. Their shift began at seven o'clock. Yehuda reluctantly picked up his cap. "Try to help him, Chemda," he said to his wife. "If you need me, send for me." Then the two men went to the factory.

Daavid laid the new clothes carefully back in the wrapping paper. Then he put his own things into his rucksack. He heard the men leave and waited until they were out of sight. Then he dropped the bag out of the window. It fell softly behind a bush.

The baby was watching his movements, and talking to him, saying "Pa, ma da." He couldn't leave Akiba without saying good-by.

He crouched down by the baby's pen and put his face close to Akiba's, with the little bars between them. "Pa, ma, da!" he said back to the baby. The baby laughed, and Daavid laughed back, the same way, so Akiba would understand. Yes, that was the best time, just as Smulik the gatekeeper had said, the best thing of all was to be a baby. "Lucky baby!" Daavid said to Akiba. "You don't know how lucky you are. Born here!"

The baby reached for his hand and held tightly to his finger.

Chemda had come into the room. "We were going to tell you anyway, Daavid," she said. He tried to stand up, but Akiba still clung to his finger. "You see," Chemda said, "he won't let go of you."

Surely, she couldn't know what he had done with his bag. She had not been outdoors so she could not have seen it. But she was almost like a mother, knowing everything a boy thought.

The baby let go of him now and turned to his mother.

Daavid told her he wanted to go to the factory. He wanted to watch the machines and talk to Yehuda.

Chemda gave him two oranges, one for himself and one for his uncle. She looked at him and smiled. He tried to look into her eyes. She was picking up the baby, and the baby grasped at her hair, and she laughed, kissing and pretending to bite the baby's hand.

"*Shalom*, Daavid," she said.

"*Shalom*," he said.

Behind the house Daavid found his rucksack; he started off where Chemda could not see him from the window. He passed quickly out of the little green strip, and across the dry, cracked wasteland, avoiding the road. He went among the low white hillocks that were flat on top as though their heads had been cut off; among them he would be out of sight.

Even though it was so early in the morning the sun was very hot. The air was heavy; he felt it pressing against his ears. There were places where the earth was cleft in deep dry gashes, so wide he just managed to jump across them. He became very thirsty, and ate one of the oranges that Chemda had given him. Then he walked until he reached the cleft where the autobus road came out of the mountains. Jerusalem was up there, among the mountains. He began to climb. He would know when he came to Jerusalem, for above the city, on the very top of the mountain, he would see the great mother of stone, holding her baby in her arms.

If he waited for a bus and got on it, he might be caught, for they might be looking for him already, and then they would take him back before his search was finished.

He kept away from the road.

After some time he was high above everything and, looking back, he could see the factory. It seemed very small, and the Dead Sea all shimmering and glistening as though it were a picture on a sheet of waving paper, or not even paper, but a sheet of cloud that could become nothingness.

Daavid guessed that he had been walking for a long time, maybe two hours. He was very thirsty again. The sun was getting high. The hills were bare stone. He sat on a stone and it was hot. He ate the second orange and saved the peeling.

Then he walked again. Below he could see the road winding on the ridge of the hill, and he tried to go the way the road was going. After a time the hills blotted out the Dead Sea behind him, and all around him were only the barren shapes, like giant waves in a frozen sea of stone. He would not stop walking. He was more thirsty than before and ate pieces of the orange peeling until it was gone.

Jerusalem could not be far, because the bus had not taken even an hour to go from there to the Dead Sea. But he was all alone in a great nowhere. He walked a little more, and then he halted, and his heart was beating hard, and it was not only because his legs were tired and he was filled with thirst, but he knew that it was because he was frightened. His fear was so great that he was not even ashamed to know he was afraid. If there were wolves and jackals here, he could not have been so afraid. But there was not a living thing. There was not even grass between the stones.

Daavid stood still. And the thought came to him that no one on earth knew where he was. Not Avram, nor Miriam, nor Yehuda Halevi, nor Maccabee. No one could reach him, no one knew where he was.

After a time he made himself walk again. He came down closer to the road. And beyond a curve he saw a watering place. There was a stone pool that looked very old, and a shepherd was there with sheep and goats, and there were also three camels. One of the camels was drinking water from the pool.

Daavid hurried to the water.

An Arab merchant was with the camels, and he stopped Daavid from drinking from the pool and gave him a jug of water that had

153

been drawn from the well beside the pool. The camel train was soon ready to go again, and Daavid took the last coins that he had in his pocket and offered them to the merchant, saying, "Jerusalem?"

The merchant seemed puzzled, and stooped down to understand better what Daavid meant. The merchant was a big man with a fleshy face. "You want to ride a camel?" he said, motioning to one of the animals.

"I have to find my father in Jerusalem," Daavid said.

The merchant did not take Daavid's coins. He looked at Daavid, and at the wilderness from which the boy had appeared, and at the wilderness that lay ahead. At last he shrugged and motioned to Daavid to mount the camel.

Daavid climbed up on the stone wall by the pool, and from there to the camel's back. The merchant took his place on his little donkey, and the camel train moved away from the well.

Daavid swayed; it was as though he were on the boat in a heavy sea. On the boat he had known he was being carried to Eretz Yisroel, even when he felt sick, and now he knew he was being carried to Jerusalem.

Below, the merchant on his donkey was singing a tune without end.

They traveled for a long time, perhaps several hours, and then, beyond three hills, Daavid saw a tower. It stood all alone, and there were clouds around it. The merchant turned and called up to him, pointing to the tower, "Jerusalem."

They passed beyond the first hill, and the second. The sun was directly before them. Daavid held onto the saddleposts. He tried to keep his eyes fixed on the tower of Jerusalem, which was becoming larger. The tower swayed.

They went farther, and as the road wound, the tower was lost, and then they left the road to take a shorter way, and came out from among rocks and were on top of another hill. The tower was on the hill, facing them; it stood above a vast long wall that rose from the rock of the hill and enclosed the city. It was a wall as high as high trees, and Daavid could see three sides of it, where it held the city, and in one corner was a great white dome, with wide, shining white courtyards around it, like a palace, and beyond there were other domes and spires.

154

He did not understand how this could be Jerusalem, for when he had come from Tel Aviv, on his way to the Dead Sea, he had changed from one bus to another, and that had been in Jerusalem, they had said, but he had not seen such a city as this. The bus had passed through a few streets of a city like other cities and then into the wilderness.

He had never in the world seen such a city as this; the domes and roofs shimmered with the sun behind them, as though this were not the same Jerusalem where he had been. This seemed a city of ancient times, and Daavid was afraid that he was not where he meant to be. And as he swayed with the steps of the camel, he thought the city would be gone, for he saw it only in the intervals of the steps, as something is seen when one is nodding but not asleep.

Then his head rolled, and he closed his eyes to keep from falling, but in the last instant he knew that the merchant had turned to him. The camel halted, and then plunged down like a sinking ship. The merchant caught hold of Daavid.

"Too hot for riding a camel," the man said. He took the boy with him on his donkey.

They rode down a winding lane, to cross the valley to the city. They passed a church in a garden, with tall dark green trees enclosing the church, and it had many high steeples, curved like pears. It was like the churches he remembered in the old country, in Poland. It was a place of the Christian fathers, the merchant said. Then they passed a hillside covered with stones for the dead. It was an old, old burial place of Jewish fathers, the merchant said.

They came to the old wall of the city and passed through a narrow gate into a narrow lane filled with shops. The merchant halted his caravan before one of these shops, and Daavid got down from the donkey. The merchant took some figs and gave them to Daavid. He pointed the way, straight ahead into the city.

Daavid tried to follow the way that the merchant had shown him, but the streets kept turning. They were narrow and crowded with people, Arabs and Jews, soldiers and people in strange clothes, women in black with their faces hidden, and men and children carrying trays of food on their heads. Donkeys and goats crowded against his legs. Daavid did not know where to go or whom to ask.

155

He kept turning through dark lanes, among shops, and people pushed against him, and he felt his head still beating with the movement of the camel walking, jarring his head at every step.

He began to walk faster. He wanted to run, and at the same time he wanted to hide in a corner and huddle against a wall. Then, as he turned into one lane from another and hesitated, not knowing whether to go up or down, he felt a smooth cool touch; someone had passed a hand over his head.

He looked up and saw two priests who had just walked by him. Daavid went up to them. Could they tell him the place where he would find the names of the fathers?

The priests studied him for a moment. They wore long black robes that touched the ground, and their heads were bare. One had silvery hair. "What a strange question," he said, and then the other priest looked down into Daavid's face and asked, "Which fathers do you mean, my son? On earth, or in Heaven?"

Daavid said, "I am looking for my own father."

The white-haired priest understood then. "The boy is lost," he said.

His companion put his hand on Daavid's shoulder and said, "You look tired, boy. We will take you to your own people."

He walked between them, and they took him up through a steep narrow lane. There were shops on both sides, and he could see down into deep cellars, where men were baking bread in their ovens, and in all the dark little shops men and boys were working. As they climbed the stone stairs of the lane, the older priest said, "On this street, long ago, the Son of Man Himself passed, on His way to His Father."

They went under a low arch and then through a long dim passage like a tunnel, and then the priests showed Daavid a doorway. This was the Jewish quarter, they said. And in this place, he would find help. They wished him well and went on their way.

Over the door, on a crumbling stone, Daavid saw the shape of an open hand, with the fingers spread, two and two together. And it seemed to him that long ago, in a game as a child, perhaps in a game that his father had taught him, he had tried to place his fingers in that position, two and two together. Daavid went through the door. Three very old men with long beards, wearing long black coats, were sitting against the wall, reading from books in their laps; their lips moved, but made no sound. There was another stone archway, with stone stairs going down into the rock. He came to a very old heavy door and pushed against it, and it opened slowly.

Inside, there was a long, cool room, like a crypt hollowed deep in the stone of Jerusalem. The cool air touched his face. He saw small windows high in one wall, and Daavid heard a singing murmuring at the far end of the room, where he saw rows of candles burning, and old, old men, like grandfathers, sitting on benches, bending over their books. Over their heads they wore striped shawls. It was a murmuring he had heard long ago, before his father had gone away.

Daavid approached the nearest of the old men, who stood against a little desk on which were two brass candlesticks and a high round box of silver, open, showing a scroll of writing.

Some of the old men had raised their heads and were looking at him, though they kept on with their murmuring, and their fingers moved down the pages of their books, as though they were looking at their books at the same time.

Daavid asked the first of the old men, "Is this the place where I can find the names of the fathers?"

The old man reflected. "The names of the fathers?" he repeated. "Here we have the names in the Torah, of Abraham, Isaac, and Jacob, Seth, Noah, and all of our father's fathers. Is this what you seek?"

The names were some of them names that he had known, and yet they also sounded strange to Daavid. "My father's name is Yisroel Halevi, from Poland," he said. Then he recalled that Yehuda Halevi had told him this name, and perhaps it was wrong altogether. But he felt so sure he remembered it. "At least I believe that is his name," Daavid added.

Nevertheless the old man seemed to understand. "The place you want is not in the old city, but in the new Jerusalem," he said. "Do you know your way there?"

"I can find my way," Daavid said.

"It is not so easy to go from here to there."

The old man went over to the benches. Now Daavid noticed there were a few boys sitting among the grandfathers. The old man approached one of them. "Yitzchak," he said, "help this boy find his way to the new city."

Yitzchak rose, took off his striped shawl, folded it, and laid it away with his book. He wore a long black coat and a round hat, and he had curls by his ears, and he was exactly the same as the pious old men, except that he was small and had no beard.

And in that moment Daavid recognized who they were, these old men. For they were the same as the old men at home, the old Jews in the ghetto in Cracow, the old grandfathers he remembered from when he was very small.

But surely he had known that all such Jews were dead.

Yitzchak led him out by another door, a low small door cut in the thick wall of the synagogue, and Daavid followed the boy through another low dim tunnel, even darker than the one by which he had come; then they went up a flight of steps; his feet felt the hollow of each worn stone. The passage was so narrow that they had to go one behind the other. All along the way Daavid saw into the tiny rooms in which people lived, and there were places where the wall dropped away and he saw down into deeper levels, and below were also places where people lived. And from one such cellar someone called, "Yitzchak, wait!"

Yitzchak called back, "I'm busy," and hurried on with Daavid.

Daavid glanced back, and, disappearing into a dim arched passageway below, he saw what looked like a tiny old man, in a long coat and with a long black beard.

They came from the stairway into a stone courtyard, where people were cooking, and two goats were tied to a door, and a little girl was rocking a baby in her lap. Then a boy with a fierce mustache like a policeman's jumped out in front of them and whirled a pair of sticks that made a strange noise. "Yitzchak, where are you going?" he called.

But Yitzchak paid no attention and took Daavid into another narrow lane, covered by low balconies that made it seem a tunnel. This was the shortest way, Yitzchak said, but then a whole group of children in a doorway blocked their path. These children, too, were strange, for they were not even like children. Daavid saw them, in the dim area behind the doorway, where there were iron gratings and stairs going down and up. Far behind was a last streak of light on that stairway, and he could see a girl, beautifully dressed in a long gown, holding a black lace parasol, like a lady. And in the doorway there was another girl, with long hair, wearing a long black gown and gloves that reached above her elbows. And from behind her peered a tiny boy, with a thick black beard, and a high black hat.

"Yitzchak! Yitzchak!" they called, laughing.

Daavid did not know what they could be. He told himself they were children like himself, and yet it was as though he did not really know who they were or what they were, whether they were children or grown people become small, or people of no age, and he did not know in what world he was.

And now another girl came into the path of light at the top of the stairs, and she was wearing a crown, with a star above her forehead. She came down toward them and said, "Yitzchak, you are Mordecai!" Then, studying Daavid, she said, "This boy can be the king!"

"I can't. I have to find my father," Daavid said.

"I have to take him to the new city," Yitzchak explained. "He doesn't know his way."

She came toward Daavid, and the others made way for her. She was surely like a queen. "I'll come with you," she said.

The other children followed her, and more and more of them came out of doorways and passageways, following Yitzchak and Daavid. The narrow lane brought them to a great wall, with ledges and ramparts, and there were still more children, climbing on the steep steps that went up the wall, or running along the narrow ledges and balancing on the parapets. Many of the children were in long coats, with long black stockings. Some of them had painted beards on their faces, and some wore long false beards. Many of them whirled the sticks that made the strange crackling noise, like breaking bones.

Daavid and all the children with him were on a long, wide flight of stairs that went alongside the wall. On the other side of the stairs were houses built one on top of another, and the stairs went up as far as he could see.

Three of the little child-men jumped out from a place in the wall and barred their way, wagging their heads with their long beards, thrusting their faces at Daavid and shouting strange words.

"Why have they got beards?" Daavid asked.

The queen was walking with him. "Don't you know it's Purim?" she said.

He did not know what Purim meant.

Yitzchak looked at him strangely, as people had looked in the woods at strangers who might be traitors. "Aren't you a Jew?" Yitzchak demanded.

The queen said, "He's not from Eretz Yisroel. He's from Europe."

Yitzchak said, "Even in Europe they know."

Then the queen explained to Daavid, "Purim is the story of Haman the Hangman."

On the wall two boys were jumping up and down, reciting a song:

"Haman, Haman, hang him high,
Fifty cubits in the sky,
He said all the Jews should die!
Save us, Esther, Mordecai!"

"Who were Esther and Mordecai?" Daavid asked.

Esther was the queen, they said, and her uncle was Mordecai. It was long ago, in the time of the Assyrians, when they invaded Palestine and took all the Jews away to Babylon as prisoners, Yitzchak told Daavid. In their land there was a king, King Ahasuerus, and in his court was the mighty Haman, who wanted to kill all the Jews.

"He ordered them to be killed," the queen said.

Now this was something Daavid knew. "Did Haman burn them in a crematorium?" he asked.

A tall boy, wearing boots and carrying a wooden sword, said, "No, they didn't have crematoriums in those days."

The queen suddenly took Daavid's hand and said, "You be the king, be King Ahasuerus!"

The tall boy cried, "No! he can't! He can't be king! He's Mordecai, the Jew!"

"A Jew can be king!" cried the girl with the parasol. "We had King Solomon and King Daavid!"

"Ahasuerus was king in Babylon," the tall boy stated. "The Jews were slaves, and he ordered them to be killed." He brandished his sword.

Suddenly Yitzchak declared, "Ahasuerus is a Jewish name. It is the name of the eternal Jew."

Daavid could not understand them. And how could he play the king?

Then two little girls ran up and knelt and seized Daavid's and Yitzchak's hands. "Save us, Uncle Mordecai! Save us, King Ahasuerus!"

They ran in front of the queen and clung to her hands. "Save us, Queen Esther!"

The boy with the long black beard cried, "I am Mordecai!" And the tall boy with the sword ran after him, and several boys whirled their wooden noisemakers and ran howling along the street, and the rest of the children shrieked, "Haman! Hang Haman!" And they ran after the boy with the sword and jumped on him and beat him to the ground. Yitzchak and the queen hurried after them. Daavid ran too, and they went through an arch in the high wall, and suddenly they were in an open street, with cars and busses, the same as in other cities he had known. On this street, people were like real people, in ordinary clothes. It was the street he had seen from the bus.

The fighters were howling over the tall boy on the ground, and all were laughing again as he crawled on all fours with Mordecai riding on his back. Then they all walked upright in the street again, with Daavid among them, singing.

A lady stopped and smiled at them. She was an older lady, wearing a large-brimmed hat that shaded her face, and there were pleasant wrinkles around her mouth. She looked at all the children, and then at Daavid, and said, "And who are you? Where is your beard? Are you King Ahasuerus or Mordecai?"

"Please," he asked her, "where is the office where they have the names?"

The woman listened, and he explained again, and Esther the Queen explained, and then the woman understood what he wanted. She said the place was not far away. She would take him there. She walked with Daavid, and all the children followed.

They came to a great building, with a driveway for cars. People were going in and out; some were dressed like officials, wearing neckties and jackets, and others were like Avram and his comrades in the settlement, wearing shorts and open shirts. Everyone looked at the crowd of children and laughed, and an official who was carrying a portfolio stopped to talk to them. The lady explained what Daavid wanted.

The man with the portfolio said, "Aha. You want the Search Bureau for Missing Relatives." He looked at Daavid carefully, and Daavid thought perhaps this man himself knew everything that was written down. "The Bureau is not here in the main building," he said. "We didn't have enough room. It's in the overflow office, across the street there. You'll see the sign."

The tall boy said, "I know! I know already!" He pushed Daavid along, and all the children followed after them, singing:

"Haman, Haman, hanging high,
He said all the Jews should die . . ."

And everybody in the street smiled at them.

They crossed the street, and went a little way down, and halted before an open yard that looked like an excavation. With his sword the tall boy pointed to a sign. "It's here," he announced.

Behind the sign Daavid saw only a war ruin. And behind the ruin was a graveyard, and behind the graveyard was the wall of old Jerusalem. He had come all the way, and found the place, and it was a bombed ruin. It was gone.

"No, Daavid," Queen Esther said, "it's not from bombs, it's not from this war. It's an old ruin that has always been here, from the old wars, the Turks, or even the Romans, from all the wars. But don't worry. You see, there are still people below, in the underground part, we are still there."

And this was true, for he saw a man coming toward them, up the steps from the ruins. The man heard what Queen Esther said and cried out, "Yes, it's here! You have found the right place." He was a very big man, bareheaded, with black hair that fell across his forehead, and he had strong hairy arms. He was wearing shorts, like a settler, and his legs were strong and hairy, too. But his eyes were wild, and his voice sounded as though it would tear down walls. "The right place, exactly," he cried again, turning and staring with them at the broken walls. "In a ruin, yes, on the edge of a graveyard, yes! Once it was a stable, and then it was a jail, and now it holds the records of the dead." He turned from the ruin to the children and spoke to them quietly. "I am the only one left of eight brothers and sisters."

Then Daavid was afraid and wanted to turn back and go away. He wanted suddenly to be at the settlement, walking with Avram in the banana grove, or to be on the beach playing with the little baby. But all the children pushed from behind and began flooding down the stairs. Yitzchak and Queen Esther said, "Come! It's here!" And they drew him down the stairway.

A man was sitting on a bench there, reading a newspaper, and watching two little children, scarcely old enough to walk, who tumbled on the grass. In the midst of the ruin there was a repaired wall with a new door in it.

A mother came out carrying a beautiful baby. The baby was playing with his mother's scarf and laughing; he had golden hair, and he waved his arms and laughed to Daavid.

Queen Esther said, "What a beautiful baby! Is he always so happy?"

"Always. He is always happy," the mother said, and she smiled at Daavid and went to put her baby in the carriage that she had left standing there.

"Hurry, Daavid. Find your father. We'll wait," Queen Esther said.

But as he started for the door the tall boy seized his arm. "He can't go! He's Mordecai the Jew! I have to hang him!"

The children began to clamor and laugh and yell. They crowded around him, some holding him, some pulling him away. Frantically Daavid freed himself and ran into the building. He heard them still chanting:

> ". . . hanging high
> Fifty cubits in the sky . . .
> . . . Mordecai . . ."

At the end of a long dim hallway a large arrow, painted on the wall, pointed to an arched stairway that led down, down, as into a dungeon.

Partway down Daavid saw a little old woman sitting on a stone ledge beside a very old man. The man was looking into a big book filled with names. The woman was crying.

Another arrow pointed still farther down.

Daavid came into a narrow vaulted room. On the walls were long sheets of paper, printed lists of names, and people were standing in front of the lists, running their fingers down the long columns.

There was a desk, and near it stood a man and woman. They had finished looking at the names.

The man said, "Perhaps there will be another list."

The woman's eyes were red. "If they haven't been found by now," she said, "they are dead, and you know it."

There was a lady behind the desk. She had a photograph of two children on her desk, to look at while she worked. Daavid asked her, "Where are the names of the families that are alive?"

She picked up a yellow book. "All the names are in this book," she said.

"Is my family there?" he asked. "Halevi?"

"Where are they from, child?"

"From Poland. Cracow."

Beyond the lady he saw a long straight wall, and the whole wall was lined, as high as the arch of the roof, with boxes filled with cards. Men and women sat at a long narrow table that went the whole length of the wall and hunted for names in the boxes of cards.

Surely there were millions and millions of names along that wall. These, Daavid thought, were the names of all the dead.

A man with his hands full of papers was going from one to another of the people who were hunting for names. He came to the last one, close to the lady at the desk, and Daavid heard her repeating "Halevi" as she searched in the yellow book.

"Halevi?" the man said after her, looking toward Daavid. "That must be the boy Avram wrote about, from Makor Gallil."

"Yes," Daavid said. Everybody knew Avram.

"Wait, Daavid," the man said. And he went away, far down the wall of names. Then Daavid saw the man halt and look over the shoulder of a white-haired woman and reach among her papers.

164

After a moment Daavid could not wait. He asked the lady, "Please, can I go in? Avram wrote about me."

She looked at him for a moment, then smiled and let him pass.

At the far end of the wall the director, Eleazer Bentov, was looking through the file of the searcher to whom he had given Avram's letter. She had completed the search. It was all there, in the blue folder. The names of the mother and baby had been found.

"They were on the Auschwitz list written down by that survivor from Cracow," the searcher reported. The director nodded. It was a list that had hitherto proved reliable. The man had worked in front of the furnaces and had secretly recorded the names of those of his townsfolk whom he recognized.

The folder contained another slip, with the names of the father, Isasschar Halevi, and a sixteen-year-old son, Samuel Halevi. These had been found in the files of the dead at Dachau.

On the full list of the family only the child Daavid had been unaccounted for.

"Did you send a report to Avram?" the director asked.

"Not yet," the searcher said.

The director wondered aloud, "Why did Avram send the boy here?"

"I don't think we can tell him," the searcher said.

It was then that Daavid approached. "You have to tell me!" he cried out. And in the same moment he snatched the papers from the man's hand. He looked at them. They were full of writing. On the blue cover he could read the name Halevi, as his father had shown him. That was all he could read.

"What does it say?" he demanded.

The director said, "We haven't found your father yet, Daavid. Nor anyone in your family. Not yet."

Daavid looked at the white-haired woman and the man. They both knew. They both knew everything.

"Then they are dead!" he cried. "If you didn't find them, they're dead, and you know it!"

They didn't say anything.

So now he knew. He knew everything.

As he climbed the dungeon stairs, the shouting met him from outside.

"Mordecai! . . ."

". . . hanging high!"

"Hang the Jews, I order it!"

"Save the Jews!"

"Where is Mordecai, to save the Jews!"

"Save us, Mordecai!"

"Ahasuerus!"

". . . hanging high . . ."

"Fifty cubits in the sky . . ."

"All the Jews should die!"

The girl with the parasol ran up to him and seized him. "Save us! Save us from Haman the Hangman!"

And the cracking noises, cracking, breaking noises . . .

"Mordecai!"

The queen took hold of his arms. "Daavid! Your father? Your mother?"

And someone said, "Did you find them?"

The boy, the man with the beard was shouting, "I am Mordecai! Who are you? I am Mordecai!"

"Who are you?" they cried all around him.

"Your father?"

"Your mother?"

"Choose! Who are you?"

"King Ahasuerus or Mordecai?"

The queen said, "Who would you like to be?"

The baby was reaching, laughing, laughing, "Mama, mama!" Such a happy baby. Always happy.

The mother's face, smiling, bending close to the baby, smiling. "Always happy!"

All around him, the girls, the mothers, their faces smiling, the fathers and grandfathers with their beards.

"Who would you like to be?"

Daavid heard them . . . riding on the camel, rocking, and on the ship on the water, rocking, and the baby in his mother's arms, rocking. . . . He smiled at them. He was rocking, and their faces were bending over him, mothers and fathers, and he smiled at them and was happy. . . .

166

They bent over him where he lay smiling on the grass.

"Baby! He's playing he's a baby!" said the girl with the parasol.

"He's mine! I'll be his mother!"

"We have to dress him as a baby!"

But Yitzchak said, "In Purim there is no baby."

Queen Esther cried, "Daavid! Stop it! You're Ahasuerus! The king!" She knelt down close and looked into his face. "Daavid! Stop pretending for a minute!"

Then the tall boy commanded, "Say something! Talk!"

They whirled the wooden clappers.

He laughed so strangely, so happily.

Then the mother saw that something had gone wrong among the Purim children. Other grown people hurried to them as she called out anxiously. Someone telephoned the Hadassah Hospital for an ambulance.

Chapter Nine

When Avram and Miriam reached the Dead Sea, late in the morning, they found Yehuda Halevi at his work in the drying plant. Daavid was at home, he told them. And then, under Smulik's stern gaze, he told them everything that had happened with himself and the boy.

As Yehuda spoke it became difficult for him to include the young woman in his confession. She made him feel more and more ashamed, as though all he had done in taking the boy to him had been weakness. There was something about her that Yehuda had already felt from among a few survivors lately come from Europe, who were working in the plant. It was a kind of rigidity. Their will was too strong. Even the child was like that. Sometimes Yehuda wondered if he himself had been like that when he had first arrived in Palestine.

But Avram, he felt, truly understood how he had come to tell the boy that he was his uncle. Avram might even agree that it would be best for Daavid to remain with the family, and might help persuade the boy. "You will see," Yehuda pleaded, "he has a home with us, just like one of the family."

Yehuda arranged to leave his work for an hour, and took them to his house. But there, Chemda said, Daavid had gone to him, in the factory. "I gave him an orange for you."

They could not look at each other.

Through the screen door they saw the gray, parched wilderness.

Chemda hurried into Daavid's room and saw now that his things were gone, and she blamed herself. "I should have understood right away!"

Yehuda blamed himself. "I should have known. I should never have left him and gone to work."

Miriam looked at the baby, sleeping so easily.

"They were already so fond of each other. Like brothers," Chemda said.

They could not think where to begin to look for the boy. On the faint chance that he might have been seen by the people of the Dead Sea settlement, they went there. But Daavid had not been seen, nor had the truck drivers from the settlement or from the potash works seen him on the road. Perhaps, they suggested, the boy had turned off at the road to Jericho, instead of following the road to Jerusalem. Or, if he had avoided the roads to avoid being seen, if he had got lost in the barren hills—

"He must have tried to go to Jerusalem," Avram insisted.

It was two hours until the next bus.

When they reached the city, they inquired of the police, for there was always the chance that he had asked his way. To go on looking for him in the streets seemed hopeless. It was already late afternoon. Then Miriam asked, "Isn't there some institution to which people might have taken him?" And suddenly Yehuda knew where the boy would have gone. "The Search Bureau!" he cried. "I should have thought of it right away! That's where he would try to go! I'm sure of it. I spoke of the place, and I kept asking about it—the place where they have all the lists of names."

168

At the bureau Eleazer Bentov kept repeating, "If you had only come twenty minutes ago!" while he nervously recounted what had happened.

"I should never have let him know what was in the folder," he blamed himself. "But he seemed to drag it out of me."

They took a taxi to the hospital.

A nurse told them the child was asleep.

Miriam asked if it would be possible to reach Dr. Alfred Mayer.

Dr. Mayer was on the hospital staff and was with the boy now, the nurse said.

They waited. Eleazer Bentov kept smoking, and each time he lighted a cigarette with his small nervous hands he was careful to offer his pack all around. His sleeves were frayed, Avram noticed, like those of all the underpaid clerks serving so fervidly in the understaffed bureaus of Jerusalem. Over and over Bentov was explaining, "I should never have spoken to the boy. When one wants to do good, it always turns out badly."

And Yehuda Halevi kept repeating, "I should never have mentioned your bureau in Jerusalem to him."

And at last Miriam, too. "I made him leave the settlement," she said. "It was my responsibility."

Avram could no longer listen to them. "Jews!" he cried out. "Have we already forgotten how it started? Have we already forgotten the source?"

They looked at him, startled, and then at each other, and then they were silent, nervously smoking their cigarettes, and seeing in horror what Avram had seen, for if it was so, it was unanswerable defeat.

Then Miriam noticed Dr. Mayer coming toward them. She recognized him at once. He did not seem older. He was as she had seen him on the lecture platform, when she had gone with Ernst to the clinic. And suddenly everything stopped within her; she felt as though an instant of paralysis had passed along her entire left side, where Ernst used to sit beside her. Then this was gone, leaving only a lingering weighty numbness, such as she had carried through all the first years.

The professor was the same. His bulging forehead, as always, seemed faintly damp, and the same thick black mustache overlined his settled mouth. It was as though he had passed through nothing—whatever the way of his escape. It was as though he had stepped from the lecture hall into this corridor, pausing only to take his white coat from a hook and put it on. It did not seem real, that there could be such a continuation.

Or, it made everything that had passed seem unreal and even nonexistent. With a sense of panic Miriam strove against the feeling that all those years, the total of all the lost, and the total of everyone's suffering, even the suffering of a child like Daavid, all could be omitted from this continuation without the slightest effect on reality.

"You are his friends," the doctor said. "Good that you have come. We can try. I hope—if he will recognize someone—" He studied each of them deliberately, as though deciding which might be his most useful instrument; and in the same instant Miriam felt that he included a fractional thought about her own being, aside from the child, and that he detected all that was in her.

He led them into the small room.

Daavid felt happy, happy. A woman's face, like a mother's, bent close to him. A beautiful scent came from her hair, and was all about her. There were bright little buttons on her dress. He touched the buttons.

She spoke to him. "Daa—viii—daa—viii." He knew the sound. It was the same sound that was always for him. He tried to make a sound for her.

A man's face, like a father's, bent close to him. There was a different odor, good and warm. He grasped the man's curly black hair. All the big people were making sounds for him. He smiled to them. He was happy with them.

Another man's face, like a father's, like an uncle's, bent close to him. The man puckered his lips, and a sound came out; it was not talking, but a pretty sound that went up and down. Daavid puckered his mouth, trying to make the same sounds, and could not, and laughed.

"We called it our family whistle," Yehuda Halevi told the doctor.

"Try it, try it again."

170

Yehuda whistled again for Daavid.

But Daavid lost interest and turned once more to Avram, reaching up and clasping his neck.

"Can he stand up?" Avram asked the doctor. "Can he move?"

The doctor said he was not certain of the precise point to which the child had regressed. But he nodded for Avram to try, and watched intently as Avram lifted Daavid in his bed.

The child stood, half balancing for a moment, holding to Avram with one hand, smiling delightedly at Avram and Miriam and all the people, as if in the discovery of a new thing he could do, and making baby-sounds of speech. Then he let go of Avram and was turning to Miriam when he wavered, lost his balance, and sat down precipitately on the bed. He was gravely startled for an instant, then burst into pleased laughter.

Miriam looked at Dr. Mayer. His intent expression never changed. He had turned from Daavid and was examining the bits of things that had been found in the boy's pockets and placed on the bedside table. There was the comb, and a little stone with the print of a seashell, and a few copper coins, and there was a crumpled folded paper. This the doctor unfolded, putting it carefully together where it was torn. He studied the picture. Then he asked Miriam, "Do you know of this? He drew this? It represents his family?"

"Yes," Miriam said. "He drew it for me."

The child saw the white fluttering thing in the hand of the being in the white coat and reached out, wanting it.

"Try it," Dr. Mayer said, giving the picture to Miriam. "You try it."

She gave it to Daavid.

He waved it, making it flutter. He turned it one way and another, and looked at it. Then he looked at them, and tossed it, and watched it fall.

"He has ended his search," Dr. Mayer said.

All around him was love. It was as though he was wrapped in a warmth that came from everyone, and would always be around him, and would always keep out everything that was pain. When they bent over him, the warmth was sweeter. When they held him, the warmth went all through him. And from one of them, with the long dark soft hair, and the other of them, with the strong curled hair, it was better than from all the others.

They looked at Daavid, and then at the doctor. In all of them was the same question. Would he remain like this?

The doctor answered slowly, with tender respect, with the awe that man must feel before a perfect and beautiful act of nature. He recognized the cruel and absolute purity of the answer that the child had found, in a child's way. Why should Daavid wish to leave the goodness that he had found, where there was infinite security and love? Why should he not cling to this?

"Then if he remains like this, doctor," Yehuda said, "will he have to stay here?"

"Or in an institution, perhaps," the doctor said.

"Can we take him with us?" Avram asked.

"For the time being," Dr. Mayer said, "I must try what I can. You see, we must try to make him leave this perfect home that he has found."

Could he leave it then? Could he come from it?

This could happen, the doctor informed them. Perhaps through a shock, perhaps gradually. "I do not know him yet. I do not know how deep the trauma is. We will try with sleep. With deep sleep."

The nurse was closing the blinds.

There was no more that they could do here. He asked them to come into his office and tell him all that they knew about Daavid.

The nurse had prepared something for Daavid in a glass, and Miriam asked if she might give it to him. Dr. Mayer nodded. She took the glass and held it for Daavid. He tried to grasp it, with both hands over hers. She guided it to his lips, and he drank, with his large eyes open, to her. Then he was content to let her lay him back upon his bed.

Miriam bent over the child to prepare him for sleep, and her movements were a resumption, a continuation of long ago. She smoothed the pillow, and tucked in the coverlet, and touched the baby's hair, and touched his eyes, saying, "Sleep, sleep, my darling," and bent and kissed his forehead.

The others were already by the door. She went soundlessly to

172

join them. And in that moment, as they reached the door, the child cried out, "Mama!"

The doctor was as quick as Miriam and Avram. He too leaned over the boy. "And mama's name, Daavid?"

Daavid felt forever enwrapped and happy again. Both faces were so near. "Mama, papa," he repeated.

Avram saw how it could be now. The child had told them himself how it could be. For with Daavid it was the same as with every being; growth would drive him outward. Only this time, as he grew, he must be made to feel his home everywhere about him.

"We must take him home with us," he said to the doctor. "We can be what he wants."

Almost reluctantly the doctor responded. "Still, it is a false situation, isn't it? A false identity." He was looking steadily at Miriam.

"It's what he wants," Avram repeated.

"And suppose," the doctor said, "some shock should come again, to remind him this is not his real self?"

"It could happen all over again," Miriam said.

"But if he begins like this with us," Avram insisted, "he can grow like a newborn child. He will be a new person, he can learn to talk and walk like any child."

"That could be true," the doctor said. "And yet, even if no disaster comes, is that what is wanted? Is that health? There is only one way for the child to grow, in health, in reality. The boy will be well only when he knows who he is, and what happened to him, and when he is able to go on from there. Yes, we have lived too much with illusions in the past."

Miriam walked with Avram from the hospital. Her being was where the child was. They walked along the ridge of Mount Scopus. On the right side, on the next hill, lay all of Jerusalem. It rose from the valley and spread beyond its walls, like a growing being that knew no barriers. The last glow after sunset melted the city all together, holding its spires and domes and towers.

173

On the left side lay all the wilderness, dropping to the Dead Sea.

The time had come to let Avram speak, it could not be put off any longer. They passed beyond the hospital, among the buildings of the university, and down to the empty stone benches of an amphitheater. They came to a balustrade looking out over the entire wilderness, and even to the dark sea.

He had brought her here, Avram said, because it was a favorite place of his.

Yes, she saw now, it was the place where all the young had to come, with their minds and their hearts beginning to live. In every university in the world there was such a place, one spot that was in itself the universe of meeting.

And she had to allow him to speak to her here.

Once the settlement had sent him to the University for a course, Avram said. And so he had found this place. He liked to look down upon the nothingness, the wilderness, and think, "Out of this we made a university." It made him optimistic.

It was the optimism of all the universities of the world. "Yes, everything seems possible, in a university," she said.

Then he tried at once to reach her. "You lived a university life once, didn't you, Miriam?"

"I told about that," she said. She began to walk, and he walked with her.

Then he tried again, more directly. "Why don't you ever talk about yourself, Miriam?" he demanded.

She answered, "Talk doesn't change anything." For it was because of the boy, and not because of herself, that they were here.

Then Avram faced her and said, "Miriam, all of you have a right to be bitter. And we have no right to criticize you. But we hoped that with us you would start to live again."

No, it was not bitterness that was in her, but how could she tell him what it was? How could anyone tell anyone?

And still he spoke to her. "After all, everyone who came here to our country began a new life. Can't you?"

"A new life? In an institution perhaps," Miriam said, "as an idiot child!"

Then Avram seized hold of her wrist and held it immovable, as it had been held that other time, and she felt each piercing word. "Don't talk like that!" he commanded her. "There is nothing wrong with you, and there'll be no institution for Daavid. We'll take him home with us. He'll grow up like a newborn boy. He'll catch up to his own age and be perfectly normal."

"Normal!" To this she had to cry out. "Yes! I tried to make him normal. A normal orphan."

"You were only trying to help him." The pressure was even stronger upon her wrist.

"No, no! It was not for him, it was for myself!" she cried. "I tried to make him give up even the memory of his parents and come to me! I drove him into this! I did it to get him for myself!"

Wasn't he done then? Couldn't he free her and let her go, with the evil in her.

She had done nothing, Avram said. "This would have happened to Daavid as soon as he found out his parents were dead whether you had sent him to the children's village or not. But now, Miriam, you can help him out of his sickness."

What did he know of sickness, being from here. "Leave us to the institutions," Miriam said. "We are the permanent cases. They know what we need."

"The boy knows what he needs!" Avram responded. "He needs a mother and a father. He made himself into an infant in order to get them. What he has done is pure nature. I have seen it in animals that know how to heal themselves when they are hurt. And our child knows what you need too. He has made you his mother." Then he challenged her, declaring, "You want the boy."

"What has it to do with what I want?" Miriam replied.

He did not spare her. "Because you once had a child," Avram said.

Then Miriam gave way. "Yes, if you must know, I want a child. I would take any child. That is how I came to hurt Daavid, and I will not do it again."

It was done and he let her withdraw her arm.

They walked under the trees. And his speaking now to her was only like the throbbing after the brand. "Miriam, you must stop being so suspicious of everything that is good for you. It's perfectly normal for you to mother Daavid."

They walked where the normal walked, the young people grown in Palestine. They walked past the buildings of arts and sciences, of chemistry, of biology, of all these things that made the normal world. From the archway of the library they looked upon Jerusalem.

Then Miriam said to Avram, "There is no use in pretending we can be normal by trying to live with substitutions. We have to live as what we are."

"But you are a woman," he said to her.

How could the healthy know the life of the amputated? Then she would have to say the last thing that would make him know. "Why do you think I survived, in Auschwitz?" she said to him. "They left only those who were in the hospital. I was in the ward for biological experiment. Daavid can have no mother and father. I can have no more children."

And still he said to her, "But you have been given this child, Miriam. We have Daavid. He has made us his mother and father."

Then she could stand it no longer. "Leave me alone!" Miriam cried out. "You want to sacrifice yourself for us, out of pity. You are one of those who feel guilty because they can't do enough for the refugees."

Avram turned away. His face was to the city as he spoke. "I suppose everyone that is still alive feels some guilt toward those of you who went through what you did, and those who were put to death. Even we who fought, we felt that we could not do enough. We kept feeling that there ought to be some way, some way to reach—I don't know, some way to do miracles, to get to our people and bring them here."

Then Miriam said, "And now you want to pay for this failure by helping me."

He turned to her once more, and as he spoke he took her wrists again, and it was as though the thing that she had been awaiting now came, for the branding had to come again, upon her second arm, just as it had been before, and now she felt the burn of the final branding, the special mark, as it was being put upon her. "As for me, Miriam," he said, "I do not come to you with pity or with guilt. I feel that after you have come out of your past a little, you and I can grow to know each other as we are. I believe I can make you come out."

No way was left now, only to twist and writhe and try with all

176

her being to escape. "I can't! I can't! I tell you I am not a woman like the others! I can only live within what's left of me!"

Avram said, "Every feeling that was mutilated in you is trying to reach out and grow. You have no right to stop what life itself is trying to do! Even when a bone is broken, it tries to grow together again. Daavid is trying to grow again in the only way his organism knows. And you, you want to destroy everything in you that makes you a woman."

"Yes. Because I should have destroyed myself," Miriam said. "Other girls were able to do it. But I wasn't able to do it."

He must see it all now. The special mark was finished, on the right hand, as well as the numbers on the left. Miriam unfastened the sleeve on her right arm, and as she raised her forearm, the cloth fell away, and the word was clear before his eyes.

"It is you who feel guilty," he said slowly, "and for no reason." What did he know of guilt?

A child could live again, he had done nothing of himself. But not she.

"I had to go on living," she said. "I had to go on living. There is no way for me to be born again."

Then Avram covered the word with his hand. "We know about this, Miriam," he said. "This, too, I have seen. You are not the only girl they forced to this. But with us, what was done with you does not exist. Only what you do with yourself exists."

She said, "What was done with me is part of me."

"I can't help you in this, Miriam," Avram said. "But our whole life here will help you if you will open yourself to it. I believe you can. I believe in you."

And she begged, "Can't you leave me alone?"

"I will leave you our child to take care of," Avram said. "He is your responsibility, Miriam. You will bring him home." Then at last he touched her no more. "I have said everything I can to you, Miriam. You must come part of the way yourself. When you want me, you will know where to find me."

Again she heard him say, "I believe in you." Then he went his way.

Chapter Ten

In Makor Gallil the youth group at last received the news they had so long awaited. They were being allotted land for a new settlement, and in the new area, the desert of the south, the Negev.

Though he was down with one of his periodic malaria attacks, Abba insisted that he had to go with Avram to inspect the site. He fretted, and stormed, while young Dvora took his temperature, and Avram laughed.

"Fever!" the old man shouted. "You know my fever never lasts longer than a woman's tears! Wait one more day. I'll be up!"

"You can come after we have built a hotel with running water," Avram said.

"What do you children know about the desert," Abba complained. "You see, you even believe there is water there!"

"If you could settle here," Dvora said, "we can settle there."

In the next bed Blaustein turned away from them; his body vibrated with fever chills, like a taut string.

After Avram and his advance party had been gone for a week, Amos drove out with Dvora, Ziona, and a few of the others to carry supplies to the boys and have a first look at the settlement site. It was a drive of many hours, but they were merry. Amos and Yehudith knew so many songs that they never repeated one during the whole journey, and Ziona taught the *sabras* songs of the concentration camps.

Finally they passed through a village of earthen huts, Beersheba, and then came a vast British military encampment. There they left the paved road and followed tire tracks over a camel path across the desert. Now at last they were coming into their land. It looked vast, with no break, no impediment to the landscape, only the slowly rolling straw-colored sand. This was where they would spend their lives. The young people fell silent. All at once they were struck with the solemnity of their task, with the formidable vow that they had made, to raise life out of this desert. They would do it, yes, for there was no alternative. But now they felt older.

Then far across the sand they saw the isolated tent. Relief came over them. At least the boys were still here. Nothing had happened to them. And Ziona said very seriously, "I've thought of a name for our settlement. Makor Chadash. New roots."

They could drive only to within a few hundred yards of the tent, for Amos feared that the truck would sink in the sand if he drove it off the slightly hardened track that had been made by British jeep patrols.

When they alighted, he kicked up a spray of sand. "I've got a better name," he said to Ziona. "Paradise."

But none of the boys had appeared from the tent; surely they should have come running forward to meet the truck. Shouldering the boxes of provisions, the gasoline tins filled with water, the visitors trudged across the sand.

The tent was empty. No one was in sight.

But then Dvora laughed out loud in relief. For a little way behind the tent she saw clumps of earth flying out of a hole. And in the hole they found Maccabee and Lazar digging furiously.

They were digging a well, they explained, to surprise Avram, who had gone off exploring. They intended to surprise him with a well full of water!

"You'll fill it with your own sweat!" Dvora laughed as she gave Maccabee a hand and pulled him up from the pit. "How do you know there is water here?"

The experts had said so, Maccabee declared—the geologists who had come a few days ago. They had examined the formations and declared there was water underground exactly at this point.

"Look! I've got the plan for our settlement." Tirza flourished a long paper roll she was carrying. "It's for Avram."

"Open it," Lazar cried, scrambling out of the well.

They spread the drawing out on the sand and studied it. "Right here," Yehudith said, looking off into space, "I'll plant an avenue of evergreens."

"They won't grow in the desert," Maccabee said expertly. "The best tree for the desert is the eucalyptus."

"They'll grow," Yehudith said. "We'll bring water, and they'll grow."

Avram returned. He looked thinner, and dark as an Arab. He glanced into the well the boys had dug and smiled. "What are you digging for? Oil?"

"Do you think the water is much deeper?" Maccabee asked.

"Not much deeper, but about a hundred yards to your right," Avram said. "Pioneers!"

Maccabee swore that the expert had pointed to this very spot.

In any case, Avram advised them with solemnity, they had better not dig any farther, for did they not know that the British had passed a regulation forbidding such excavations? What a calamity it would be if oil were to be discovered on the grounds of a Jewish settlement! Then the Jews, like the Arabs, would possess oil, and the British would not know whom to favor.

But did the experts really think water could be found here? Amos demanded.

"Water? There is water everywhere," Avram said. "You have only to catch hold of it." It was not a well that the geologists had indicated, but the site of an ancient *haraba,* a cistern dug in the ground, for storing rain water. They had found traces of this. Yes, people had lived here before, the land had been fertile. And what people they had been! "There are the remains of a whole irrigation system out there," he said. "And look at this!" Avram held up a little stone that he had found; it was a carving of an animal, with long ears and a long nose. A goat, Yehudith declared, because of the wise look on its face, but Dvora was sure it was a cow, because of its round heavy form. Avram said it could be only a donkey. Then they fell to discussing their plans.

"Who's coming up in the first group?" Maccabee asked.

The list was ready. Yehudith gave it to Avram.

"Let's see these pioneers." One by one Avram went over the names. "Weisbrod?"

"He wanted to come so much," Dvora pleaded. "We made him the secretary. He can take care of the storeroom and everything."

"Besides, he can turn in a good day's work now," Amos said. "You should see him harnessing the mules."

180

It was true. Avram had himself noticed that, like so many of the sickliest looking survivors, Weisbrod possessed surprising energy. And there was another consideration. Even though the man had completely gone away from his life as a doctor, even though he would probably forever refuse to use his knowledge again, still it was there. And in an isolated colony, as this would be, it was better to have such a man than not.

Avram let Weisbrod pass. But then he came to Miriam's name. "Isn't she still in the sanitarium with Daavid?" he asked. "Is he better?"

Dvora had been to see them. Daavid was a little better, she said. He could sit up by himself, and, though he could not speak, she was certain he understood nearly everything that was said to him. He did not seem to comprehend a word of Yiddish or Polish, but only Hebrew, she said, as though he had been born in Palestine. Miriam was working in the sanitarium, so as to be with the boy.

"But now I think they ought to come home," Dvora concluded.

Maccabee agreed. "We ought to have them here with us."

They waited for Avram's approval.

"Do you think you can carry such a burden from the very beginning?" Avram asked. "Surely you realize that no settlement brings children along in the first period. And Daavid is a helpless child."

"Besides," Amos pointed out, "he is receiving treatment at the sanitarium."

"It would be better for him to be with us now," Dvora insisted.

"Aside from what is best for the boy," Avram said slowly, "there is the question of Miriam." Squatting on the sand, he looked into the circle of their faces as they sat by the pit. "Your group is a shock troop," he reminded them, "laying the foundation of a new settlement, an outpost. You will be isolated, and live close together. Each person must be chosen for the life of the group. You will not be able to make allowances for people who are immersed in themselves."

As he spoke, they saw themselves as they would be, pressed in upon each other in the little cabin that would be their dining-room and the center of their lives; they saw themselves at night, entirely isolated, and dependent on each other to keep off the loneliness of the distance around them, the whole desert.

"I've seen it happen," Avram said, "that one such person can destroy the morale of an entire group."

Then Maccabee said, "That's right. Miriam—she never makes me feel that she is one of us."

"Maybe this is just what would help her," Dvora said.

Amos pointed out that they were already taking along Weisbrod.

"She can come later," Lazar suggested. "With the second group. Then it would also be safe to bring Daavid."

"Does everyone agree?" Maccabee said, relieved.

All but Avram and Lazar were going back to Makor Gallil to prepare for the day of settlement. Avram walked to the truck with the young people. "Till Thursday," he said.

And as they were leaving, Avram gave Dvora the little stone animal he had found, to take to Daavid.

Nahama and Shulamith came up to Jerusalem and brought Avram's gift to the sanitarium for Daavid.

Daavid was sitting up now, on the large sun-soaked veranda, and Miriam was feeding him. Shulamith ran toward him, crying, "*Shalom,* Daavid! We came up on the milk truck."

Daavid turned to her, smiling, and she was sure he understood, but her mother reminded her, with a little shake of the head, "Shulamith—"

"Yes, I know," Shulamith said. "Daavid is sick and can't talk. Won't you talk to me, Daavid? Your little sister Shulamith?"

There were toy building blocks on the little table beside him, and he beamed at her and gave her one of his wooden blocks.

"How is he?" Nahama asked Miriam.

"He's much better," Miriam said. "He can almost feed himself now." And she let Daavid take the spoon.

He took it in his fist. "Daavid," Shulamith cried, "is that the way you hold a spoon?" She grasped his hand and arranged the fingers correctly on the spoon, and Daavid used the spoon properly. They laughed together, delighted at what they had accomplished.

182

"Everyone asks for him," Nahama said to Miriam. "Doesn't Dr. Mayer think he can come home now?"

Miriam did not respond at once. Then she said she thought, since the child was showing improvement, it would perhaps be best to keep him where he was.

"Is Dr. Mayer still giving him sleep treatments?" Nahama asked.

"No." Miriam explained that since Daavid had not come out of the long periods of sleep with any memory of his former self, Dr. Mayer had given up the treatment, "For the time being Dr. Mayer believes the best thing for Daavid is relaxation and good care," Miriam said.

"Mother, let me give him his present," Shulamith demanded, and Nahama brought out the little stone animal from her handbag. "It's from Avram," Nahama explained to Miriam. "He found it on the site of the new settlement. People lived there once, but now it's an absolute desert. In the Negev."

Shulamith put the toy into Daavid's hand. "Avram sent it to you, Daavid," she said. "From the Negev. It's a donkey!"

The boy turned the toy in his hands and studied it.

"Avram and some of the youngsters went up in advance," Nahama said. "The settlement is going up on Thursday. Yehudith is taking every plant, every tree we have in the nursery. Avram must be planning a whole colonization, not an outpost. They say he's been working like ten men."

"Who is going there?" Miriam asked.

Nahama studied her. "Young Dvora, Maccabee, Ziona, even Weisbrod. Blaustein is broken-hearted—he has to wait because of his malaria. Swobodniak has left for the city. But Amos, Yehudith—fifteen of the youth group and fifteen of your group."

Daavid was playing with the donkey and repeating, "Avram, Avram."

"Listen to him!" Shulamith cried.

Nahama and Miriam watched Daavid. He held up the toy to Miriam, but this time with a clearly different meaning. "Mama, Avram?" he demanded.

The great preparations for going out to the new settlement were already nearly completed when Miriam arrived at Makor

Gallil. As the milk truck drove through the yard, as far as the infirmary, she saw two extra trucks, borrowed from other settlements, standing ready, loaded with farm implements, ladders, provisions, fodder. The yard was frantic with activity as the new settlers hurried toward the trucks with the last, almost forgotten necessities—cots, straw mattresses, benches, tools. Weisbrod was loading a wheelbarrow on Chayim's truck, while Zev lamented that it was not actually on the transfer list.

Natan, the driver of the milk truck, helped Miriam carry Daavid inside.

The little hospital was not free of the excitement that pervaded Makor Gallil, and now, with the coming of Daavid, all the sick seemed ready to jump out of their beds, calling, *"Shalom! Shalom,* Daavid! *Shalom,* Miriam!"

Abba left his bed and would have taken the boy from her arms. "Daavid, Daavid, do you know me?" he insisted. "Abba?" The child recognized him and repeated, "Abba, Abba."

Daavid was excited and would not rest, though he had until now slept regularly every afternoon. He recognized Blaustein, and even seemed to know the Yemenite girl, Bathsheba, who brought him bananas and milk. But at last he began to drowse, holding the little donkey to his face and muttering the name of Avram.

Nahama said she would sit a while with the child, and Miriam went out into the yard.

Zev and Weisbrod called *shalom* quite as though things were unchanged, and returned to their game of wrangling over their list. For Weisbrod was now dragging an ancient plow to load on the truck. He had changed, in the month of her absence; he looked younger, and even cheerful.

"Are you following the proverbs of Solomon?" Zev demanded, and quoted, " 'We shall fill our house with spoils.' "

Weisbrod calmly hoisted up his loot. "Solomon also said," he retorted, " 'Cast thy lot among us—we shall have one purse.' "

Grinning, Zev gave the looter a hand with the plow, and Miriam caught herself feeling light with pride over Weisbrod.

Most of the young people were packed and waiting for the moment to climb into the trucks. There was a holiday atmosphere in the yard. The new settlers came out of the dining-hall and soon

they were dancing the *horrah*. A cousin of Amos, Ben-Yosef, had
come from Afikim with his accordion, and already the circle
swung around, their arms outspread and entwined, their hands on
one another's shoulders, their knees rising high, and their feet
smacking the earth as they chanted:

> *"Chai! chai!*
> *Am Yisroel chai!*
> *Am Yisroel chai!*
> The nation Israel lives!
> The people Israel lives!"

From every side dancers hurtled into the circle—newcomers,
comrades, cousins, even several comrades from the *Hannah
Szenesch* who had been sent to other settlements, and young
pioneers from other settlements, and comrades taking their noon
rest, from every side they broke in, opening a link, entwining their
arms left and right, and binding the circle together again, never
missing a step as they chanted, and the circle absorbed them all,
growing, swinging faster.

> *"Chai! chai!*
> Israel is alive!"

Dvora, dancing in the circle, saw Miriam and called to her,
"Miriam! You've come! Come and dance, Miriam!"

Miriam waited until the circle brought Maccabee toward her.
She motioned to him. The lad failed to understand her for a moment, then dropped out of the dance, coming awkwardly to her.

"Maccabee," she asked, "can you put us on the list for the new
place? Is there room for us there?"

Stammering, the boy said, "Well, Miriam, we wanted you in
the first group, but it was decided—because of the conditions it
was decided—"

"I've brought Daavid," she pleaded. "It will be the best thing
for him, to be with the people he knows. I'll take care of him and
do my share of work too."

Maccabee struggled. Surely she understood that no settlement
ever brought out children at the very first. And it had therefore
been decided—

"Who decided?" she asked.

"We. We decided."

"You? You didn't want me?" Miriam demanded.

"I? I would have been for, but—"

"Dvora? Ziona?"

"In the beginning we even put you on the list. But Avram—"

"Avram!"

"It was a vote," Maccabee said. "The vote was against."

Even in the hospital the beat of the music was inescapable: . . . alive! . . . alive!

Abba was sitting on his bed, swaying to the song. "Who is boss," he demanded, "a germ, or Abba? How can they set up a colony without me?"

It was useless to try to restrain him. "Go, kill yourself," old Zipporah said from her bed. "Only let us have quiet here."

As though this were all the authority he needed, Abba rose from his bed and seized his clothes.

Nahama was still sitting with Daavid. He slept fitfully and had not let go of the little stone image. He kept asking for Avram, Nahama said.

"Yes, I know." Miriam felt the woman watching her, with that patience and understanding that was sometimes almost insufferable; like an accusation.

Then Miriam said, "I talked to Maccabee. They would take Daavid. I'm sure they would. No matter how difficult it would be. It's me they don't want."

Nahama did not reply.

The child slept, and they went out together toward the dancing. The song had changed.

"Come, come build the Negev!" they were singing.

"Come, come build the south!"

And finally, Miriam asked Nahama, "Why don't they want me?"

"Perhaps, Miriam," Nahama said, as though she had been waiting for the question, "it's only because you won't let anyone feel you want them." Nahama's fingers took hold of hers, and Miriam hesitated to break the clasp. "We are friends, comrades here. It's a way of living together, not apart."

Abba was already among the dancers. He would kill himself. He plunged around the circle, hoarsely chanting the same song, but with the words as they had been in his day—"Come, come build Galilee!" And the youngsters outshouted him, "Negev, Abba, Negev!"

Once more Abba swung past Miriam. "Miriam, come and dance!" he shouted.

A smaller circle broke off, formed within the large one, and circled counterwise. Someone shouted the first notes of a new song, and the song changed again, without a moment's halt:

> "Joy! joy!
> . . . yes we must
> Learn joy!"

Dvora broke out from the dance and ran to Miriam, pulling along a tall young man in uniform. "Miriam! It's my brother Shlomo! He's come!"

"Miriam, come and dance, Miriam!" the brother insisted, laughing.

Zev whirled by in the circle, lifting his legs, stamping his feet to the earth.

> ". . . joy!
> Yes, we must,
> Must, yes, we must . . ."

"Nahama! Miriam!" Zev called. "Come and dance!"

Dvora and her brother were caught, whirled back into the circle.

"Miriam! Nahama! Come!"

Zev's long arm reached for them, and Nahama whirled in, and Miriam was pulled along with her.

For a moment Miriam didn't know. The circle carried her, forced her into its swing.

> ". . . must,
> Yes, we must
> Learn joy!"

Her arms were intertwined, and she scarcely knew who was on one side of her and who on the other. Then the words were coming from her, too, joined with all the others.

187

The trucks moved out in a row. Hanging on them, encrusted on them, on their implements and on their plows, were the young settlers, singing "*Am Yisroel Chai.*"

There was an assembly point, at a colony near Beersheba. It was a drive of six hours, through the length of Palestine, and they arrived after dark. The heavier trucks, laden with sectional cabins, were already waiting. And there Avram waited to assemble his section of the Hagana. At midnight they mounted the trucks again. Avram's group went in the leading vehicle. Each man carried a stout walking stick in his hands. In some of their pockets emergency weapons were ready. The truck carried fenceposts, coils of barbed wire, sledgehammers, and digging tools.

There was no more singing. The trucks proceeded without lights. They arrived in darkness. The settlers leaped from their vehicles.

Amos, Avram, Zev, and all the men of the defense groups quickly placed the fenceposts around the perimeter.

Chayim and Maccabee swung sledgehammers on the posts.

Ziona and Amos carried a roll of barbed wire between them on an iron bar. They unrolled it as they walked.

Each group unloaded its truck. The big cook tent was unfolded. Ben-Yosef and Lazar shouldered the poles, and a dozen comrades came to pull on the guy-strings, to set up the tent.

Tirza and Bathsheba carried in the pots, the loaves of bread, the provisions. They set up an outdoor stove, to cook for the crowd of helpers and friends who would come for the raising of the colony.

All this in the dark, in the predawn.

Then each whispered to the other, to look, not to miss the sunrise their first time on the desert. The sky was patterned and streaked with the clouds of early morning. The clouds were from Egypt, Amos said, from the overflow of the Nile, for they were at the southern end of their land, near the Egyptian border.

All the settlers waited for an instant, halting in their labor, as the rim of the sun became visible.

Maccabee and Dvora carried concrete blocks from the heavy truck, foundation stones for the first cabin to be erected, the communal dining-hall. They put their stones down in a row, and

Dvora held the ball of string while Maccabee sighted the line for the foundation.

Avram, Zev, Hillal, Lazar, Weisbrod, another Zev, Dov, and another Dov, Ephraim, Ziona, and another Ziona, and they were all the same, there was no knowing one from another, with their bare arms, their bare legs, the short-haired girls and the girls with their braids wound around their heads, the boys in jerseys and the boys bare to the waist, two together and four together they carried the sections of the cabins, the sections of the roofs, the floors, the windows.

Then Avram heard a sound that was distant but unmistakable. It was the regular coughing of a tractor. "It's not ours," he said to Zev. And they knew that Arabs were plowing. The land had not been touched as long as could be remembered, but now someone had sent out a tractor, and the soil was being turned over, to establish a claim. The two men looked at each other, and said nothing. Such things had to come, but they had not expected the struggle to appear so soon here.

From the horizon a few long-legged camels came toward them. These were lean, swift camels of the desert; their saddles were tasseled, and their bells sang. The Arabs were nearly black, and their beards were pointed, and they were as brethren who had not departed from this place in thousands of years.

Avram exchanged greetings with them, and they watched, letting their eyes rest on the trucks, and the half-built houses, and the swarm of builders. Then they spoke of other sections of land, not far away, from which a few squatting Bedouin might be induced to depart, for a price that was not very great. And indeed it would be fertile land, they said, for since the Jews were coming, there would soon be water.

From nowhere, from out of the sand, a few Arab children appeared and ran beside the trucks as they backed and wheeled in the sand, and at last jumped and rode along on them as they departed for more loads.

Then with the full morning other comrades came, a truck load from Gvuloth, and a youth group from Rehovoth; from all corners of Palestine friends came to help with the building. Zev and Yehudith, Lazar and Tirza, and young people from everywhere lifted whole sections of walls and set them in place.

It was the day of building, the day of going up on the land. There was no trouble, and the stout clubs were laid aside.

By noon the first cottages were standing on the desert, and the tin sheets of their roofs blazed like signal mirrors as they were hammered into place.

Chayim had returned with his truck to Makor Gallil for a load of seedlings and household things. The children had prepared all the seedlings, and they came in a long line, each child carrying his plant to the truck, and Zipporah handed the plants up to Abba.

Jamal came also, with Mustafa, on this important day. They brought with them a sheep and a ram, and the small donkey, Balaam.

To Abba, Jamal presented the sheep and the ram. "With the blessings of Allah," Jamal said, "for your new house."

"Live for a hundred years, Jamal," said Abba. "For as our father Solomon said, 'A neighbor near is better than a brother far off.'"

It was sad that the new people had to go away from this place to take land in the desert, Jamal said, while good soil lay by the river, untended and barren.

Sad it was, Abba agreed, but more new people would come, and one day a way would be found for the purchase of this land by the river, and it would surely be planted.

Then they saw Chayim coming with Miriam. Chayim was carrying Daavid on his back, and he brought him to the truck.

"Here is Balaam, he is yours," Mustafa said to Daavid. "You will be well, Daavid. You will ride on him, all over Palestine."

Daavid saw them. He knew them. He knew the grandfather, and the little girl; he had known her already, in the other place where everyone was in white. She had given him the toy from Avram. He knew the donkey. It walked better than before. It was a baby and it was growing and it walked strongly. He knew the boy Mustafa, and his father Jamal. He knew the truck, the farmyard, the immense haystack, the children carrying seedlings in their arms, and suddenly he felt all this, felt the thrusting trees and the thrusting limbs of the donkey and all the thrusting within his body as though he must grow, as though he must suddenly be grown among them all.

And yet he was afraid, and could not. He clung to the man who was carrying him.

They put him in the truck, and Abba held him on his lap. Miriam was sitting close, she was the one who was always with him, but now he began to know that she was someone else, too, she was Miriam.

Everyone waved and shouted, and the truck drove out of the yard. They were going to a new place.

Avram and Weisbrod were plowing. There was no tractor yet, and they began with mules that had been brought from Gvuloth. The sandy surface of the earth flowed under the plow like water, but they set the plow deep, until it bit well into earth that was solid, and in that solid earth there were stones. Weisbrod plowed, and Avram dug out the stones. Some of them were large, and it seemed to Avram that their surfaces had surely been shaped.

Then the plow struck again, and Weisbrod turned it aside, and Avram saw a rock that was larger than the others. This was surely a building stone from an old house. Avram dug carefully around it, and then knelt, and found the corners with his hands, and pulled it up from the ground. The stone was unbroken and only slightly marred. There was carving on it.

Weisbrod left the plow and watched as Avram rubbed the earth from the stone, cleaning it carefully. A design emerged. First there was the gazelle of the desert. And then came the shape of a harp. This was the priestly harp, the sign of the Levite tribe, which served in the temple, making music. And there was also an inscription on the stone.

Avram picked the earth out of the graven lines, and the letters of the inscription became clear. It was a curious and awesome thing to find, for they were the letters of the name of an ancient Hebrew house—Halevi.

Avram shouldered the stone and carried it to the yard of the new settlement.

When the truck arrived again, Yehudith ran for her seedlings. She would plant her row of trees.

Abba lifted Daavid on his back and carried him to the yard. As Avram was setting down his stone, he saw his father carrying the boy, with Miriam walking beside them. "Daavid!" Avram cried out. "Look!"

Carefully Abba set the boy down on his feet, on the ground, steadying him.

Daavid ran to Avram. He knew Avram. He knew him from the boat, and from the beach when Avram had given him the jacket with the sergeant's stripes, he knew him from the brook where Gideon's men had been chosen.

He ran, though his legs were numb after sickness. "*Sholom*, Avram!" he called.

"Look at this stone, Daavid! See what I found in the earth here!" Avram cried as he pressed the child to his side.

Daavid knelt and touched the stone. He traced out the letters—Ha-le-vi.

They were all gathered around him, Abba, Shulamith, Nahama, Zev, Miriam . . . grandfather, sister, aunts, uncles, mother, father. . . . Looking up at them, he read the name again—Halevi. "That was the name of my real father," Daavid said.

He was safe now, Miriam knew. He would not go back. He had found all of his fathers, in their place.

"We'll build our house on this stone," Avram said.

"The house of Halevi," Miriam said to Daavid.

Daavid put his hands on the stone. "The house of my father, Yisroel."